COLLINS
HANDY ROAD ATLAS
BRITAIN

CONTENTS

2 **Key to Map Symbols**

3-49 **Road Maps at 9 miles to 1 inch**

50-61 **Urban Area Maps at 4 miles to 1 inch**

50-51   Southampton, Portsmouth, Cardiff, Bristol

52-53   London and M25

54-55   Birmingham

56-57   Nottingham, Stoke-on-Trent, Leeds/Bradford, Sheffield

58-59   Liverpool, Manchester

60-61   Tyneside, Teesside, Glasgow, Edinburgh

62-80 **Index to place names**

Collins Handy Road Atlas Britain

Collins
An Imprint of HarperCollins*Publishers*
77–85 Fulham Palace Road, Hammersmith, London W6 8JB

© HarperCollins*Publishers*

Printed in Great Britain by Bath Press Colourbooks, Glasgow

ISBN 0 00 448271 9   CDNE   HC8110

KEY TO SYMBOLS

ROAD INFORMATION

motorway

motorway tunnel

junction number

service area

primary route

'A' road

'B' road

other road

distance in miles

gradient

toll

OTHER TRANSPORT INFORMATION

railway

car ferry

airport

CITIES, TOWNS AND VILLAGES

built-up areas

settlement

Scale: approx. 9 miles to 1 inch

0   10   20 miles

0   10   20   30 km

1 : 550 000

OTHER FEATURES

national boundary

national / regional park

forest park

woodland

beach

marsh

canal

lake , dam and river

height in metres

TOURIST INFORMATION

place of interest

feet	metres
2950	900
2295	700
1640	500
985	300
657	200
328	100
0	0
	land below sea level
	water

ADDITIONAL INFORMATION ON URBAN AREA MAPS PAGES 50-61

interchange

roundabout

tourist railway

heliport

long distance path

ancient monument

battle site

camping / caravanning

castle

country park

garden

golf course

historic house

historic house and garden

information centre   all year   seasonal

motor racing circuit

museum

nature reserve

race course

religious building

viewpoint

wildlife park

youth hostel

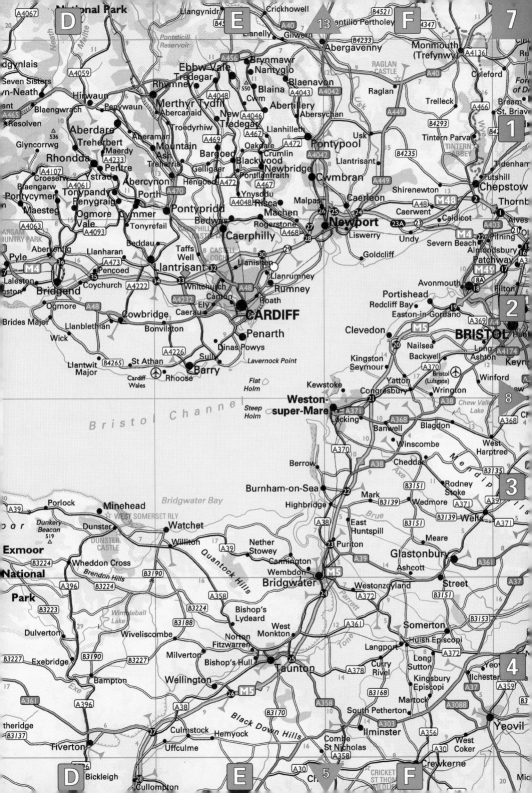

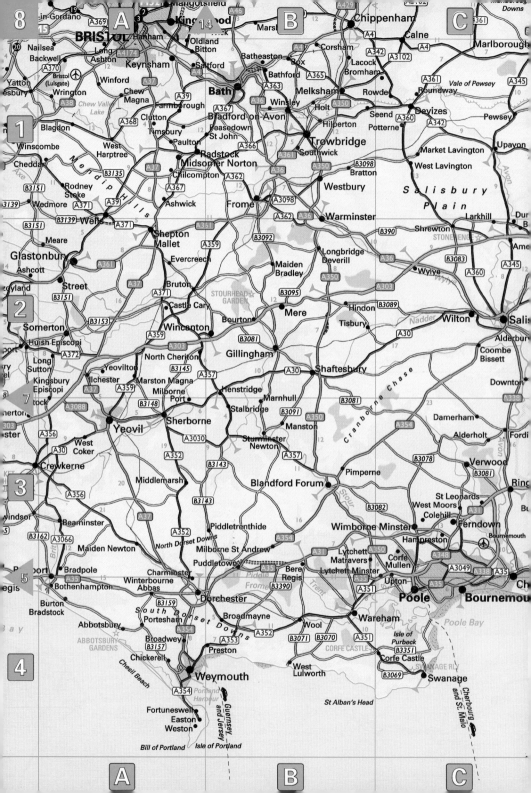

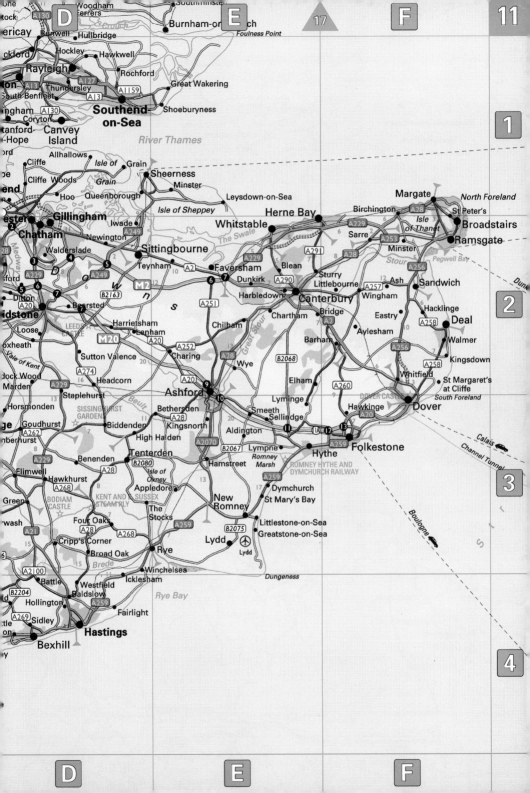

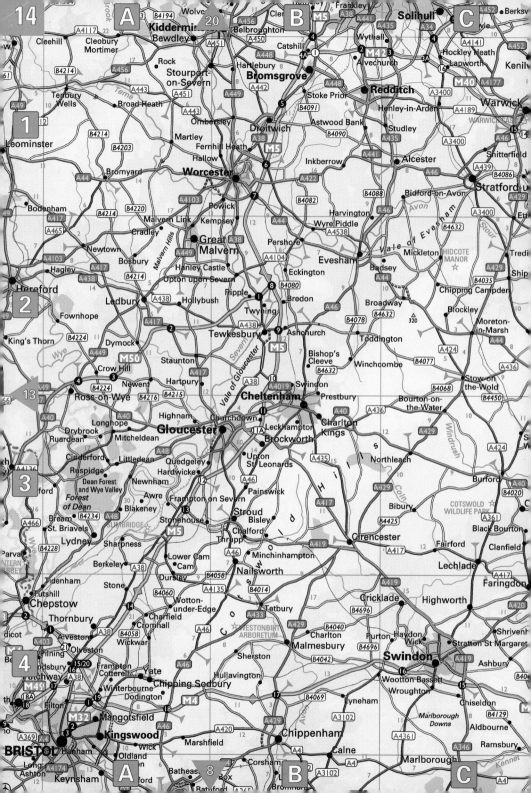

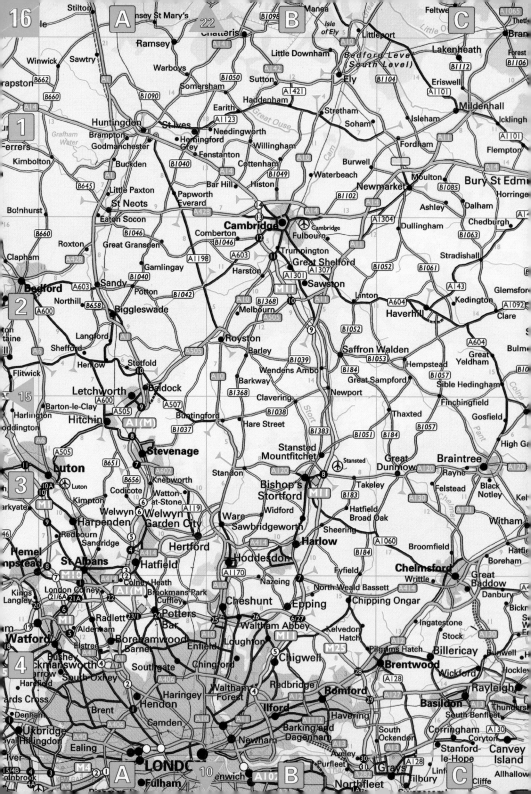

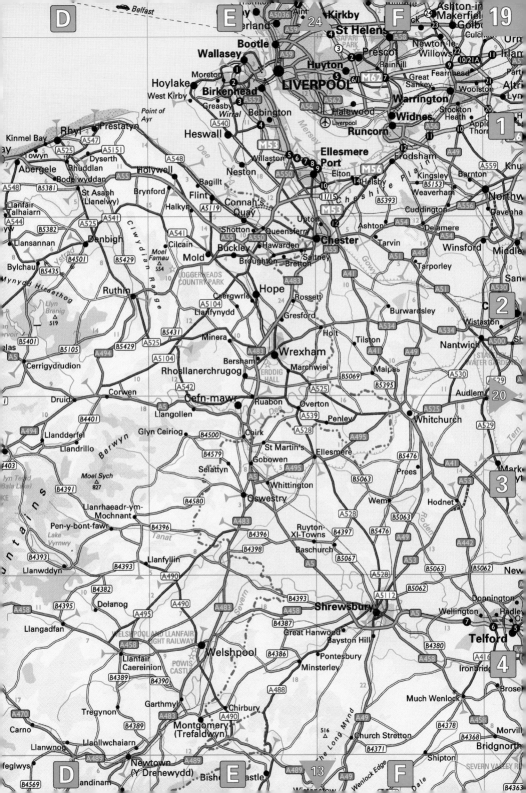

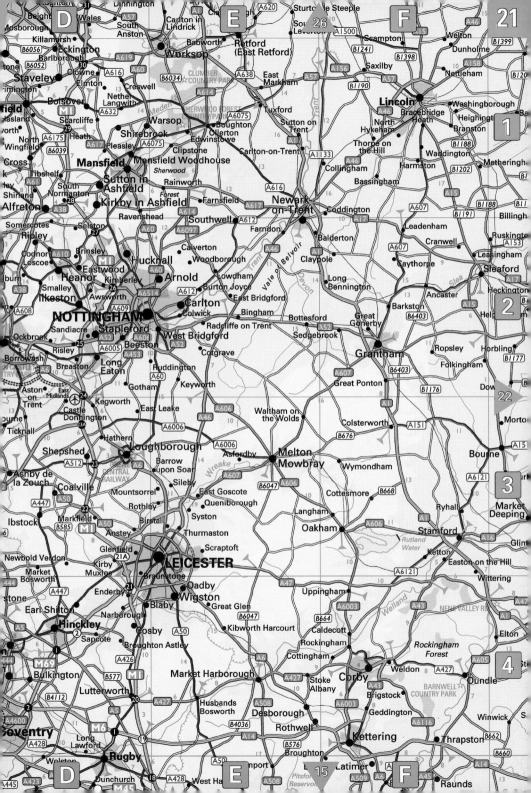

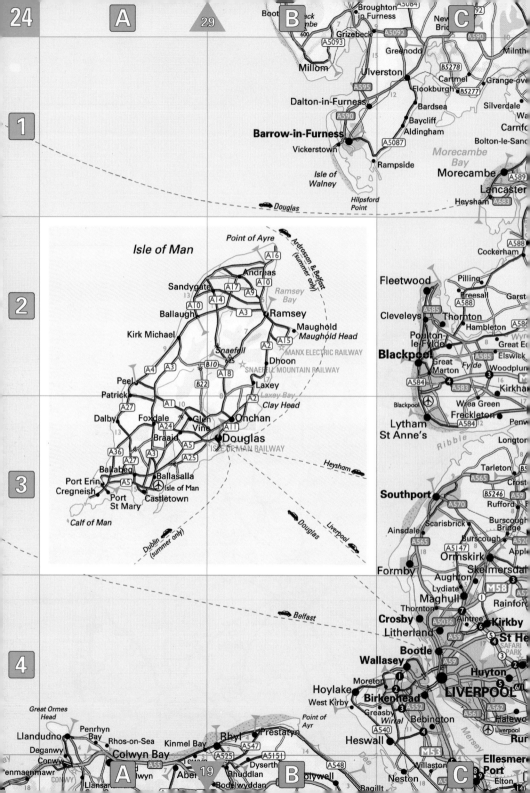

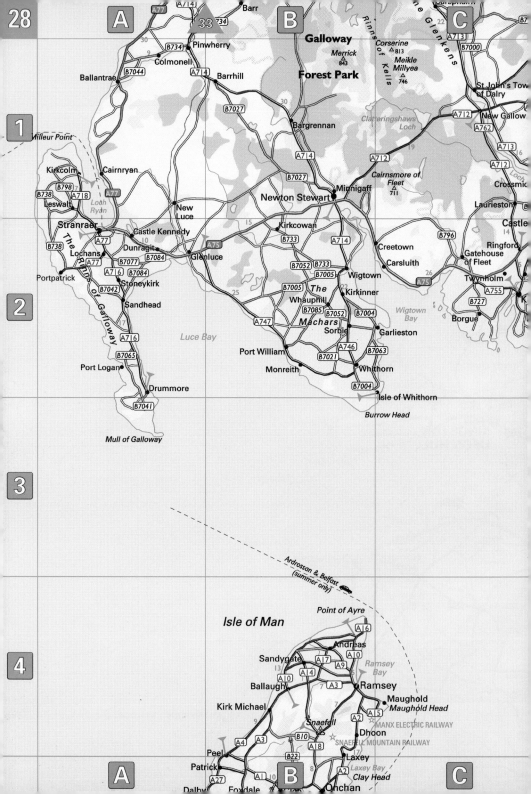

Lynemouth
Newbiggin-by-the-Sea

Blyth

ramlington
Seghill
Seaton Sluice
Seaton Delaval
Whitley Bay
Shiremoor
benton
Wallsend
Tynemouth
North Shields
South Shields

Jarrow
Hebburn
A194
Cleadon
Boldon
A1018

Sunderland
A123
Sunderland

Washington
A182
Chester-le-Street
A690 A1018
Bournmoor

ughton
Spring
Hetton-
le-Hole
Murton
Seaham
South Hetton
A182
Haswell
Easington Colliery
rham
Easington
Sherburn
Thornley
Peterlee
Horden
Wheatley
Hill
Blackhall Colliery
urn
Wingate
A1086

Trimdon
A179
Hartlepool
Fishburn
A19
Tees
Bay
Ferryhill
A1(M)
ton
Sedgefield
A689
ewton
ycliffe
A66
A689
A78
Billingham
Redcar
A77
A1085
Middlesbrough
South
Bank
Marske-by-the-Sea
Saltburn-by-the-Sea
Stockton-on-Tees
Eston
Brotton
Eaglescliffe
B1269
Skelton
Tees-side
A67
Thornaby-
on-Tees
A171
Loftus
Hinderwell
Egglescliffe
Roseberry
Topping
Guisborough
A174
Sandsend
Yarm
A172
B1366
Whitby
22
rth
ees
Great Ayton
Danby
A171
High
Hutton
Rudby
Stokesley
Great
Castleton
Sleights
B1416
Hawsker
A67
B1264
Broughton
Egton
Robin Hood's Bay
13
B1257
NORTH
YORKSHIRE MOORS
North
Cowton
A19
A172
Round Hill
RAILWAY
20
A167
8
454
Staintondale
Brompton
19
North York Moors
A171
A684
Rosedale Abbey
Cloughton
orthallerton
Romanby
A167
North York Moors
A169
Burniston
Leeming
Gillamoor
Lockton
Hackness
North Riding
A168
National Park
Forest Park
Scalby
A165
Knayton
Kirkbymoorside
Wrelton
Scarborough
A167
B1257
Boltby
Helmsley
A170
Pickering
Sproxton
Seamer
Snainton
Thirsk
Sowerby
Wass
26
Thorn
Dale
East
dkirk
7
Cayto

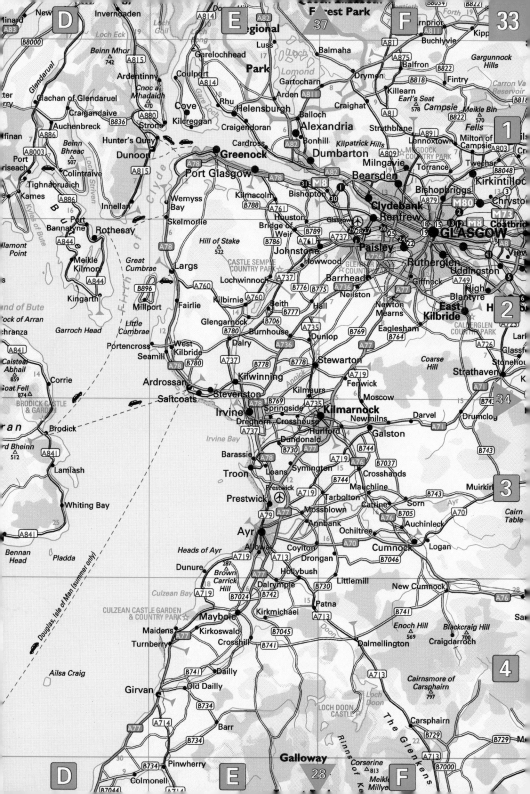

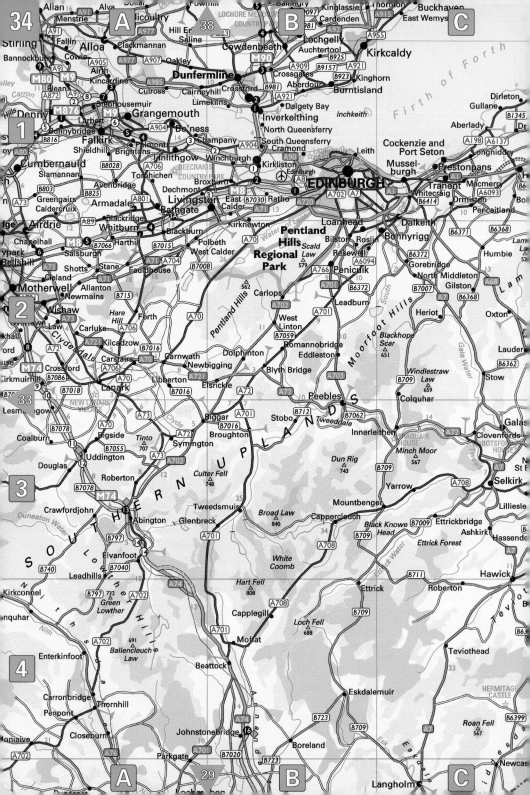

A

40

B

Rum
(Rhum)

Kinloch

C

Point of Sleat

1

Rubha nam
Meirleach

Askival
△
812

Sound of Rum

Cleadale

Eigg

An Sgurr
△
393

Galmisdale

Sound of Eigg

Sound of Ar

Eilean
nan Each

Muck

Eilean
Shona

Ockle

Ardtoe

B8

2

Eilean Mor

Point of
Ardnamurchan

Achosnich

Achara

A r d n a m u r c h a n

Kilchoan

B8007

Ben Hiant
△
528

Glenbeg

B8

Sorisdale

B8072

Clabhach

B8071

Coll

Arinagour

Ardmore Point

Glenborrodale

Glen

Loch
Eatharna

Gunna

B8070

Caliach
Point

Tobermory

B8073

Drimnin

Mo

Crossapol
Bay

Calgary

Dervaig

Loch
Frisa

Killundine

Lo
Arie

Hough Bay

B8068

B8069

Caolas

Calgary Bay

Kilninian

A848

B849

Fiuna

Tiree

B8065

Scarinish

Treshnish Isles

Loch Tuath

Salen

A849

23

Barrapol

Hynish Bay

Gometra

Ulva

Lagganulva

B8035

Knock

De
Gh

Balephuil

Balemartine

Little
Colonsay

Loch Na Keal

M u l l

Loch
Ba

Staffa

Balnahard

Ben More
△
966

3

B8035

Glen More

Ben Buie
△
717

IONA ABBEY

Iona

Fionnphort

Loch Scridain

Pennyghael

Loch Buie

Sound of Iona

Bunessan

A849

35

Carsaig

Ross of Mull

Soa Island

Ardchiavaig

Malcolm's
Point

Fi

4

Garvel

Scar

Kiloran Bay

Rubh' a' Geodha

Colonsay

Kiloran

Scalasaig

Kilchattan

Loch Staosnaig

A

32

B

arvard

C

inn Bhreac
△
467

A

47

B

C

Loch Claidh

799 (A859)

Loch Bhrollum

An Tairbeart
(Tarbert)

A859

Caolas Scalpaigh

Shiant Islands

Greenstone Poi

Rubha Reidh

Cove

Melvaig

B8021

B8057

Pooley

Gairloch

*Eilean Scalpaigh
(Scalpay)*

*ann a Deas
a Hearadh
(… arris)*

25

East Loch Tarbert

Roghadal
…nish Point

Little Minch

Rubha Hunish

Kilmaluag

A855

19

Staffin Bay

Balgown

Staffin

Vaternish Point

*Loch
Snizort*

Idrigil

Uig

A856 (A87)

Trotternish

Culnaknock

A855

Sound of Raasay

Rona

Port Henderson

B8056

Redpoint

Redpoint

Fearnmore

Lower
Diabaig

Loch Torridon

Inveralligar

Shieldaig

Ben Geary
284

Dunvegan Head

Borreraig

Milovaig

46

Lusta

Loch Dunvegan

B886

Bernisdale

A850

DUNVEGAN CASTLE

Dunvegan

*Healabhal
Bheag*
488

Roskhill

8

Loch Bracadale

B884

B885

Skye

Carbost

Borve

The Storr
719

Kensaleyre

Portree

4

9

B883

Brochel

Raasay

Oskaig

Clachan

Beinn Bhan
896

Applecross

Toscaig

Loch Kishorn

Bracadale

Portnalong

A863

B8009

Carbost

13

Talisker

Beinn Bhreac
445

Glenbrittle

*Cuillin
Hills*

Sgurr
Alasdair
993

Loch Brittle

(A87) A850

Sligachan

11

Peinchorran

Sconser

Scalpay

Luib

*Crowlin
Islands*

Bla Bheinn
(Blaven)
928

A850

(A87)

Broadford

Torrin

Duirinish

Kyle of Lochalsh

Balmacara

Loch Alsh

(A87)

Kyleakin

A850

6

Breakish

A851

Kylerhea

Glenelg

*Beinn na
Seamraig*
561

Beinn S…
98

Hebrides

Canna

Cuillin Sound

Soay

*Loch
Scavaig*

Elgol

B8083

17

Loch Eishort

Sleat

Teangue

A851

Loch Hourn

Ladhar Bh
1020

K n o y…

Mea…

Sound of Canna

Kilmory

CLAN DONALD CENTRE

Ardvasar

Aird of Sleat

Point of Sleat

Sound of Sleat

Mallaig

Morar

*Rum
(Rhum)*

Kinloch

…skival
812

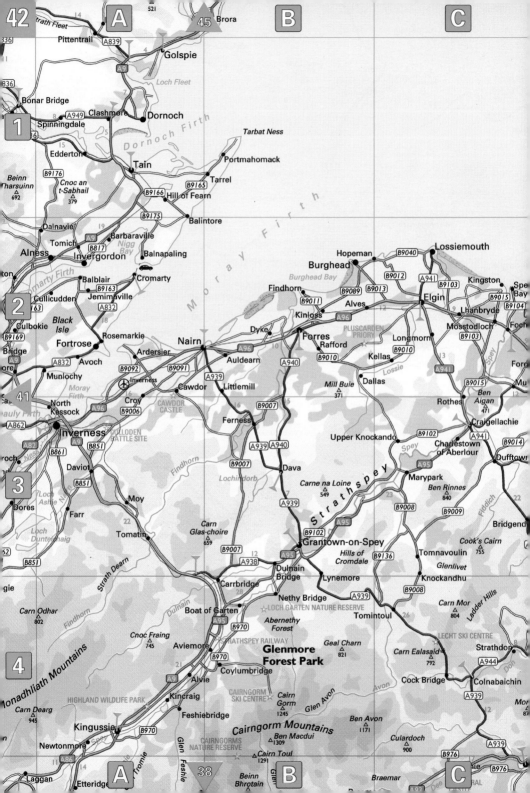

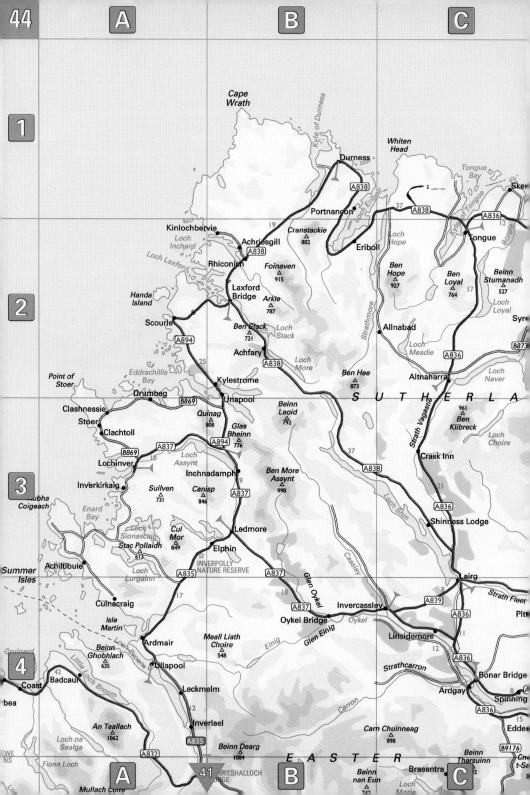

Pentland Firth

D E F

1

2

3

4

Strathy Point

Strath Halladale

Strath of Kildonan

Dunnet Head

Island of Stroma

Swona

Burwick

Brough Ness

Pentland

Scrabster

Thurso Bay

Brough

Mey

Barrock

Dunnet

John o' Groats

Duncansby Head

Strathy

Melvich

Dounreay

Buldoo

Reay

Thurso

Castletown

Loch Heilen

Freswick

hill

Halkirk

Loch Calder

Roadside

Keiss

Reiss

Noss Head

Sinclair's Bay

Olgrinmore

Spittal

Watten

Loch Watten

Bilster

Westerdale

Mybster

Badlipster

Wick

C A I T H N E S S

Loch More

Thurso

Achavanich

Camster

Thrumster

Ulbster

Forsinard

Lybster

Latheron

Kinbrace

Morven △ 706

Scaraben △ 626

Dunbeath

Latheronwheel

Newport

Borgue

Kildonan Lodge

Berriedale

Helmsdale

Lothmore

Ben Horn △ 521

Loch Brora

Brora

Rogart

Golspie

Loch Fleet

Dornoch

Tarbat Ness

Portmahomack

Tain

Tarrel

Dornoch Firth

n Fearn

Helmsdale

A836 A882 (A9) A836 A882 A895 (A9) A9 (A836) A897 A9 B871 B874 B870 B876 B870 A839 B916 B9165 B9175 A961

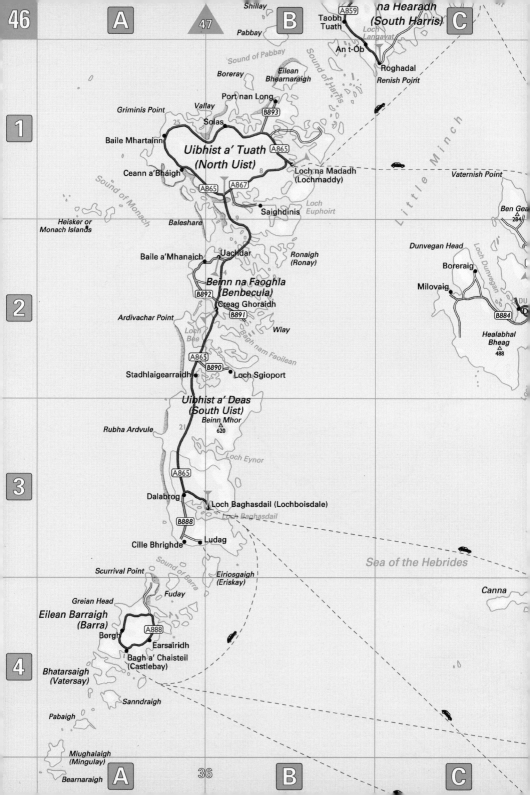

A **47** B C

na Hearadh
(South Harris)

Shillay
Pabbay
A859
Taobh
Tuath
Loch
Langavat
An t-Òb
Roghadal
Renish Point

Boreray
Eilean
Bhearnaraigh
Sound of Pabbay
Sound of Harris

1

Griminis Point
Vallay
Port nan Long
B893
Solas
Baile Mhartainn
25
**Uibhist a' Tuath
(North Uist)**
A865
Ceann a'Bháigh
A865
8
Loch na Madadh
(Lochmaddy)
Vaternish Point
A867
Little Minch

Sound of Monach
Baleshare
Loch
Euphoirt
Saighdinis
Ben Gea
284

Heisker or
Monach Islands

Dunvegan Head
Boreraig
Milovaig
Loch Dunvegan

Baile a'Mhanaich
Uachdar
Ronaigh
(Ronay)

**Beinn na Faoghla
(Benbecula)**
B892
Creag Ghoraidh
B891
Wiay

2

Ardivachar Point
Loch
Bee
A865
Stadhlaigearraidh
B890
Loch Sgioport

B884
Healabhal
Bheag
488
Bagh nem Faoilean

**Uibhist a' Deas
(South Uist)**

Rubha Ardvule
21
Beinn Mhor
620
Loch Eynor

3

A865
Dalabrog
Loch Baghasdail (Lochboisdale)
B888
Loch Baghasdail
Cille Bhrighde
Ludag

Sea of the Hebrides

Scurrival Point
Sound of Barra
Eiriosgaigh
(Eriskay)

Canna

Greian Head
Fuday
**Eilean Barraigh
(Barra)**
Borgh
A888
Earsairidh
Bagh a' Chaisteil
(Castlebay)

4

Bhatarsaigh
(Vatersay)
Sanndraigh

Pabaigh

Miughalaigh
(Mingulay)
Bearnaraigh

A **36** B C

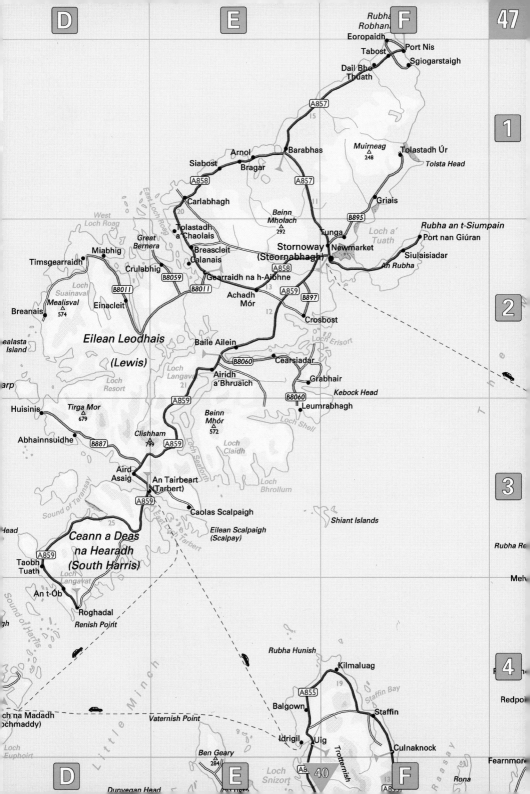

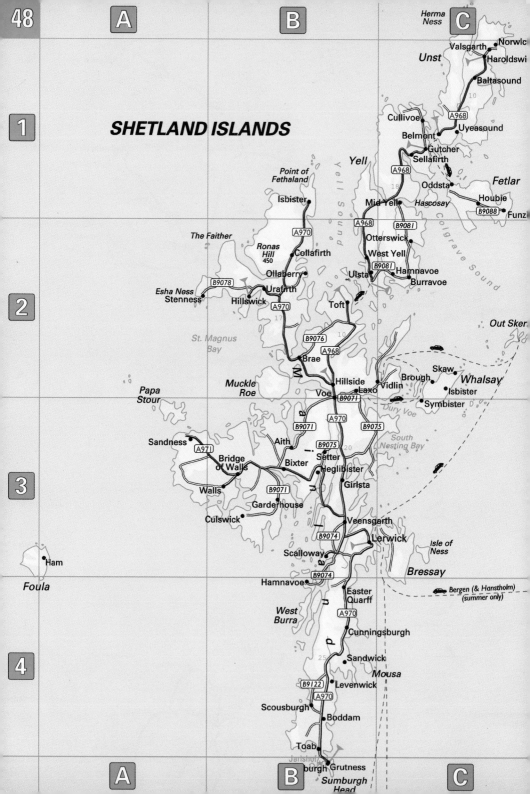

SHETLAND ISLANDS

48

Herma Ness
Valsgarth • Norwic
Unst
Haroldswi
Baltasound
A968 10
Cullivoe
Belmont Uyeasound
Gutcher
Yell Sellafirth
A968 Oddsta
Fetlar
Point of
Fethaland Mid-Yell Houbie
Isbister *Hascosay* B9088 Funz
The Faither A970 West Yell
Ronas B9081
Hill Collafirth Otterswick
450 Ollaberry Hamnavoe
B9078 Urafirth Ulsta Burravoe
Esha Ness Stenness Hillswick B9081
Hillswick A970 Toft *Out Sker*
B9076
St. Magnus A968
Bay Brae
M Skaw
Muckle Hillside Brough *Whalsay*
Papa *Roe* Voe Laxo Vidlin Isbister
Stour B9071 Symbister
A970 *Dury Voe*
B9071 B9075
Sandness Aith B9075 *South*
A971 Setter *Nesting Bay*
Bridge Bixter 20
of Walls Heglibister
Walls Girlsta
B9071 Veensgarth
Gardenhouse A970
Culswick B9074 *Isle of*
Scalloway Lerwick *Ness*
B9074 *Bressay*
Hamnavoe
• Ham Easter *Bergen (& Hanstholm)*
Quarff *(summer only)*
Foula A970
West Cunningsburgh
Burra
Sandwick
Mousa
B9122 Levenwick
A970
Scousburgh
Boddam
Toab
Jarlshof burgh Grutness
Sumburgh
Head

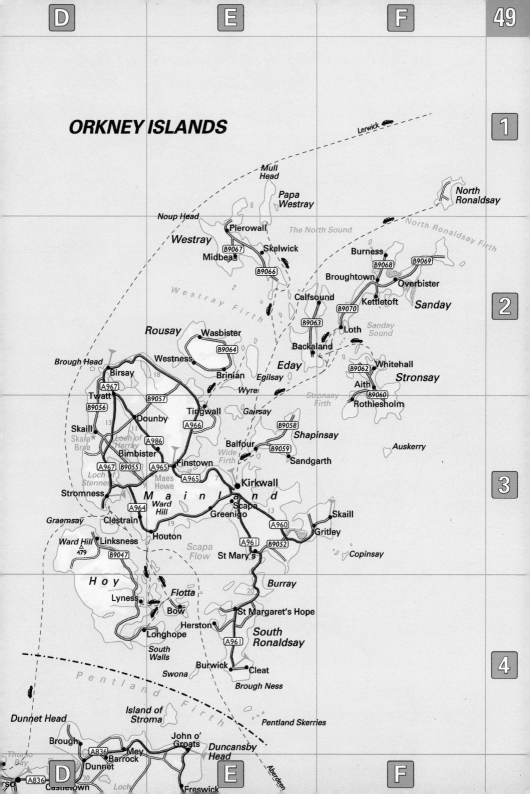

1

ORKNEY ISLANDS

Lerwick

Mull Head

Papa Westray

North Ronaldsay

Noup Head

The North Sound

North Ronaldsay Firth

Pierowall
Westray
B9067
Skelwick
Midbea
B9066

Burness
B9068
B9069
Broughtown
Overbister
Kettletoft
Sanday
Calfsound
B9070
B9063
Loth

Sanday Sound

2

Westray Firth

Rousay
Wasbister
B9064
Westness
Brinian
Backaland
Eday
Egilsay

Wyre
Whitehall
B9062
Stronsay
Aith
B9060
Rothiesholm

Brough Head
Birsay
18
A967
Twatt
B9056
Dounby
B9057
Tingwall
A966
Skaill
Skara Brae
13
Loch of Harray
11
Bimbister
A986
A967
B9055
Finstown
A965
Gairsay
Shapinsay
B9058
Balfour
B9059
Sandgarth
Auskerry

Stronsay Firth
Wide Firth

3

Loch of Stenness
A965
Maes Howe
7
Kirkwall
Stromness
A964
Clestrain
Ward Hill
19
Houton
M a i n l a n d
Scapa
Greenigo
13
A960
Skaill
Gritley
A961
B9052

Graemsay

Ward Hill
△479
Linksness
B9047
Scapa Flow
St Mary's
Copinsay

H o y
Lyness
Flotta
Bow
20
Burray
St Margaret's Hope
Herston
South Ronaldsay
Longhope
A961
South Walls
Burwick
Cleat
Swona
Brough Ness

4

Pentland Firth

Dunnet Head
Island of Stroma
Pentland Skerries

Brough
A836
Mey
Thurso Bay
Barrock
Dunnet
20
John o' Groats
Duncansby Head
Aberdeen

Castletown
Freswick
Loch

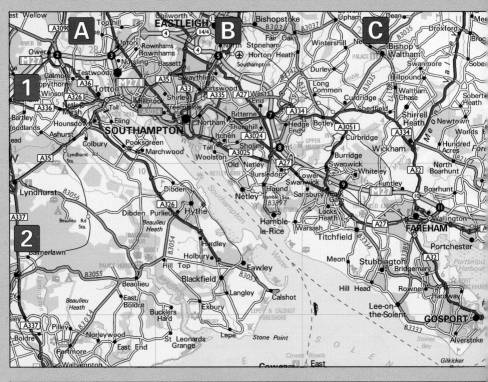

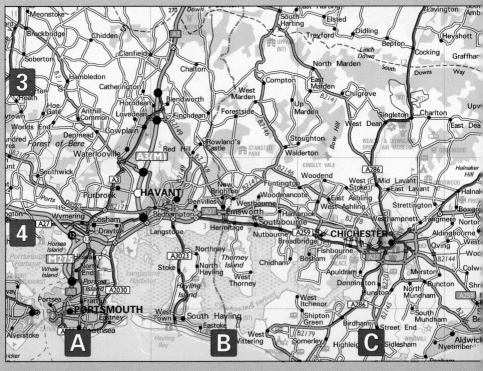

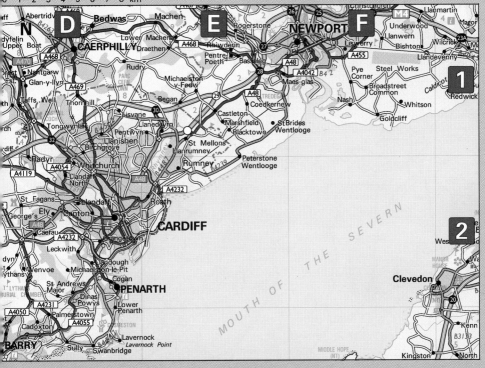

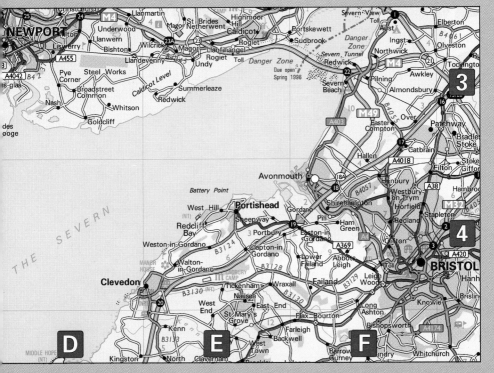

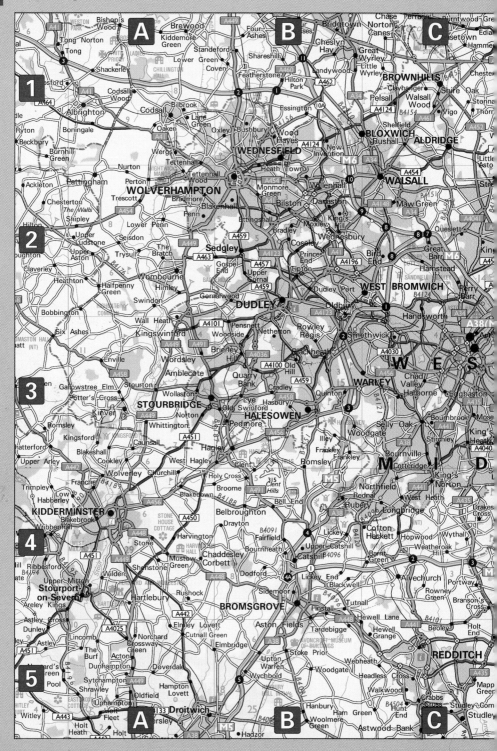

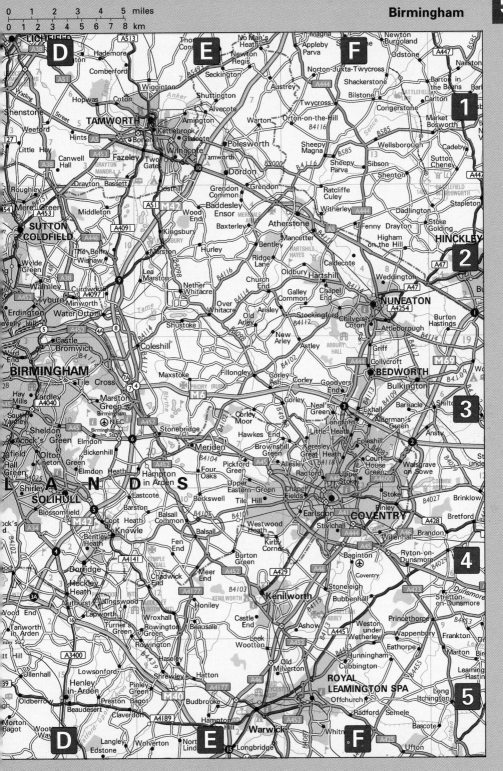

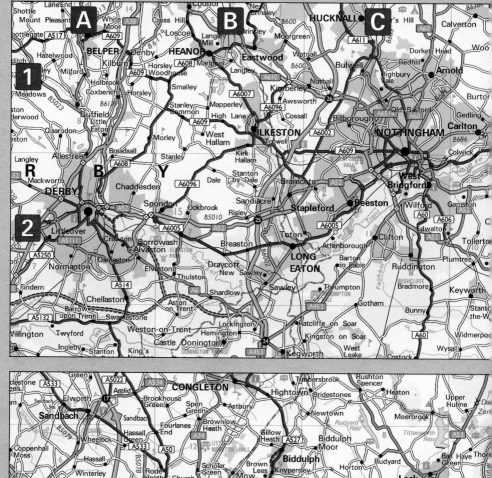

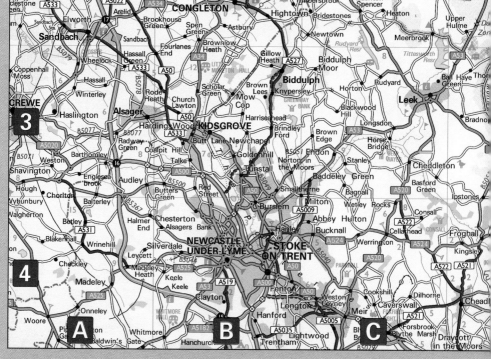

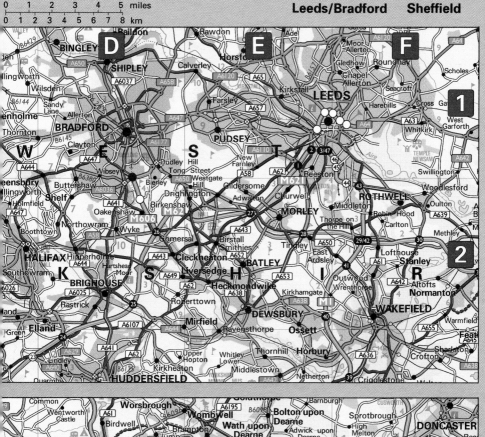

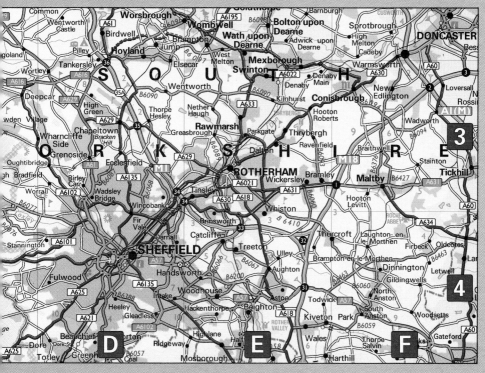

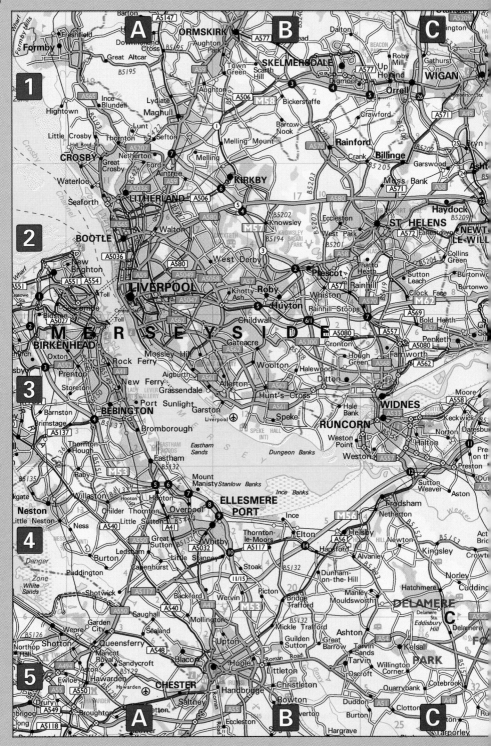

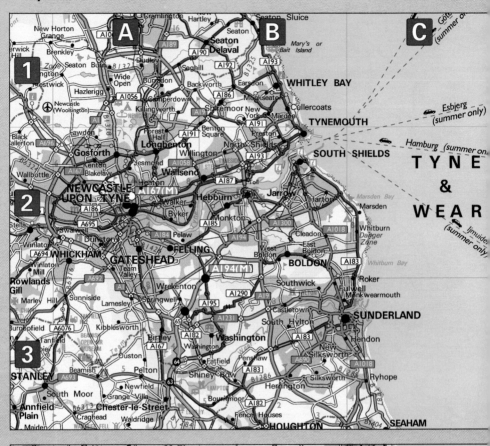

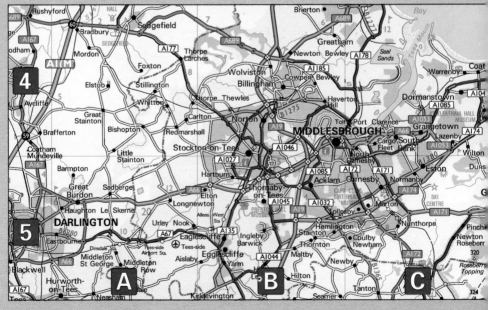

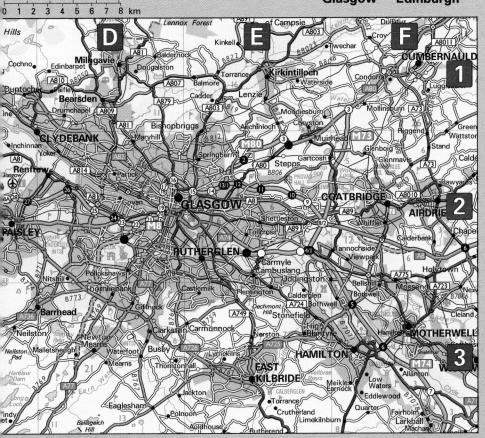

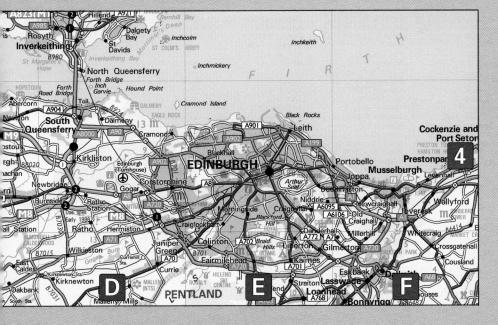

INDEX TO PLACE NAMES

Abbreviations

Aber.	Aberdeenshire
Arg. & B.	Argyll & Bute
Beds.	Bedfordshire
Berks.	Berkshire
Bord.	Borders
Bridg.	Bridgend
Bucks.	Buckinghamshire
Caerp.	Caerphilly
Cambs.	Cambridgeshire
Ches.	Cheshire
Cornw.	Cornwall
Cumb.	Cumbria
D. & G.	Dumfries & Galloway
Derbys.	Derbyshire
Dur.	Durham
E.Ayr.	East Ayrshire
E.Dun.	East Dunbartonshire
E.Loth.	East Lothian
E.Renf.	East Renfrewshire
E.Riding	East Riding of Yorkshire

E.Sussex	East Sussex
Edin.	City of Edinburgh
Flint.	Flintshire
Glas.	City of Glasgow
Glos.	Gloucestershire
Gt.Lon.	Greater London
Gt.Man.	Greater Manchester
H. & W.	Hereford & Worcester
Hants.	Hampshire
Hart.	Hartlepool
Herts.	Hertfordshire
High.	Highland
I.o.M.	Isle of Man
I.o.W.	Isle of Wight
Lancs.	Lancashire
Leics.	Leicestershire
Lincs.	Lincolnshire
Mers.	Merseyside
Middbro.	Middlesbrough
Midloth.	Midlothian
Mon.	Monmouthshire

N. & P.T.	Neath & Port Talbot
N.E.Lincs.	North East Lincolnshire
N.Lan.	North Lanarkshire
N.Lincs.	North Lincolnshire
N.W.Som.	North West Somerset
N.Yorks.	North Yorkshire
Nhants.	Northamptonshire
Nhumb.	Northumberland
Norf.	Norfolk
Notts.	Nottinghamshire
Ork.	Orkney
Oxon.	Oxfordshire
P. & K.	Perthshire & Kinross
Pembs.	Pembrokeshire
R. & C.	Redcar & Cleveland
R.C.T.	Rhondda Cynon Taff
Renf.	Renfrewshire
S.Ayr.	South Ayrshire
S.Glos.	South Gloucestershire
S.Lan.	South Lanarkshire
S.Yorks.	South Yorkshire

Shet.	Shetland
Shrop.	Shropshire
Som.	Somerset
Staffs.	Staffordshire
Stir.	Stirling
Stock.	Stockton-onTees
Suff.	Suffolk
Surr.	Surrey
T. & W.	Tyne & Wear
V. of Glam.	Vale of Glamorgan
W.Isles	Western Isles
W.Loth.	West Lothian
W.Mid.	West Midlands
W.Suss.	West Sussex
W.Yorks.	West Yorkshire
Warks.	Warwickshire
Wilts.	Wiltshire
Wrex.	Wrexham

Abbey Hulton **56 C4**
Abbeytown 29 E2
Abbey Wood 53 **F4**
Abbots Bromley 20 C3
Abbotsbury 8 A4
Abbots Langley 52 **C1**
Abbots Leigh 51 **F4**
Aberaeron 12 B3
Aberaman 7 D1
Aberavon 6 C1
Abercanaid 7 E1
Aberchirder 43 D2
Abercynon 7 E1
Aberdare 7 D1
Aberdaron 18 A3
Aberdeen 43 F4
Aberdeen (Dyce) Airport 43 E4
Aberdour 34 B1
Aberdyfi 12 C1
Aberfeldy 38 B2
Aberffraw 18 A2
Aberfoyle 38 A4
Abergavenny 7 E1
Abergele 19 D1
Abergynolwyn 12 C1
Aberkenfig 7 D2 .
Aberlady 34 C1
Aberlemno 39 E2
Aberporth 12 A3
Abersoch 18 A3
Abersychan 7 E1
Abertillery 7 E1
Abertridwr 51 **D1**
Aberuthven 38 C4
Aberystwyth 12 C2
Abhainnsuidhe 47 D3
Abingdon 15 D4
Abington 34 A3
Aboyne 43 D4
Abram 25 D4
Abram 59 **D1**
Abridge 53 **F2**
Accrington 25 E3
Achadh Mór 47 E2
Achahoish 32 C1
Acharacle 36 C2
Achavanich 45 E2
Achfary 44 B2
Achiltibuie 44 A3
Achintee 41 D3
Achnacroish 37 D3
Achnasheen 41 E2
Achosnich 36 C2
Achriesgill 44 B2
Acklam 60 **B5**
Ackworth Moor Top 26 A3

Acle 23 F3
Acock's Green 55 **D3**
Acomb 30 B1
Acton *Gt.Lon.* 52 **C4**
Acton *H. & W.* 54 **A5**
Acton Bridge 58 **C4**
Adderbury 15 D2
Addingham 25 F2
Addington 53 **E5**
Addlestone 10 A2
Addlestone 52 **B5**
Adel 57 **E1**
Adlington 25 D3
Adwalton 57 **E2**
Adwick le Street 26 B3
Aigburth 58 **A3**
Ainsdale 24 C3
Aintree 24 C4
Aintree 58 **A2**
Aird Asaig 47 D3
Aird of Sleat 40 B4
Airdrie 34 A2
Airdrie 61 **F2**
Airidh a'Bhruaich 47 E2
Airth 34 A1
Airton 25 E1
Aislaby 60 **B5**
Aith *Ork.* 49 F2
Aith *Shet.* 48 B3
Akeld 35 E3
Albrighton 20 B3
Albrighton 54 **A1**
Alcester 14 C1
Aldbourne 14 C4
Aldbrough 27 D2
Aldeburgh 17 F2
Aldenham 16 A4
Aldenham 52 **C2**
Alderbury 8 C2
Alderholt 8 C3
Alderley Edge 20 B1
Alderley Edge 59 **F4**
Alderman's Green 55 **F3**
Aldershot 9 F1
Aldingham 24 C1
Aldington 11 E3
Aldridge 20 B4
Aldridge 54 **C1**
Alexandria 33 E1
Alford *Aber.* 43 D4
Alford *Lincs.* 22 B1
Alfreton 21 D1
Allanton 34 A2
Allanton 61 **F3**
Allendale Town 30 B2
Allenheads 30 B2
Allerton *Mers.* 58 **B3**
Allerton *W.Yorks.* 57 **D1**

Allesley 55 **E3**
Allestree 56 **A2**
Allhallows 11 D1
Allnabad 44 C3
Allonby 29 E2
Alloway 33 E3
Almondsbury 14 A4
Almondsbury 51 **F3**
Alness 42 A2
Alnmouth 35 F4
Alnwick 35 F4
Alresford 17 D3
Alrewas 20 C3
Alsager 20 A1
Alsager 56 **A3**
Alsagers Bank 56 **B4**
Alston 30 A2
Altnafeadh 37 F2
Altnaharra 44 C2
Altofts 57 **F2**
Alton *Hants.* 9 F2
Alton *Staffs.* 20 C2
Altrincham 25 E4
Altrincham 59 **E3**
Alva 38 B4
Alvanley 58 **B4**
Alvaston 56 **A2**
Alvechurch 14 B1
Alvechurch 54 **C4**
Alvecote 55 **E1**
Alveley 20 A4
Alves 42 B2
Alveston 14 A4
Alvie 42 A4
Alyth 39 D2
Ambergate 21 D2
Amble 35 F4
Amblecote 20 B4
Amblecote 54 **A3**
Ambleside 29 F4
Ambrosden 15 E3
Amersham 15 F3
Amersham 52 **A2**
Amesbury 8 C2
Amington 55 **E1**
Amlwch 18 B1
Ammanford 6 C1
Ampthill 15 F2
Amulree 38 B3
Ancaster 21 F2
Ancroft 35 E2
Ancrum 35 D3
Anderton 59 **D4**
Andover 9 D1
Andreas 24 B2
Angle 12 A2
Angmering 10 A4

Anlaby 27 D3
Annan 29 E1
Annbank 33 E3
Annfield Plain 30 C2
Ansley 55 **E2**
Anstey 21 D3
Anstruther 39 E4
Ansty 55 **F3**
An t'Ób 47 D4
An Tairbeart 47 E3
Anthill Common 50 **A3**
Antrobus 59 **D4**
Aoradh 32 A2
Appleby-in-Westmorland 30 A3
Appleby Magna 20 C3
Appleby Parva 55 **F1**
Applecross 40 C3
Appledore *Devon* 6 B4
Appledore *Kent* 11 E3
Appleton Thorn 19 F1
Appleton Thorn 59 **D3**
Appley Bridge 25 D3
Apsley 52 **B1**
Apuldram 50 **C4**
Arbirlot 39 E3
Arbroath 39 E3
Arclid **59 E5**
Ardchiavaig 36 B4
Arden 33 E1
Ardentinny 33 E1
Ardeonaig 38 A3
Ardersier 42 A2
Ardfern 37 D4
Ardgay 44 C4
Ardleigh 17 D3
Ardlui 37 F4
Ardlussa 32 B1
Ardmair 44 A4
Ardminish 32 B2
Ardmolich 37 D1
Ardnadam 33 E1
Ardrishaig 32 C1
Ardrossan 33 E3
Ardtalnaig 38 A3
Ardtoe 36 C2
Ardvasar 40 C4
Arinagour 36 B2
Arisaig 36 C1
Arkley 52 **D2**
Arley 59 **D3**
Armadale 34 A1
Armitage 20 C3
Armthorpe 26 B4
Arncliffe 25 E1
Arnisdale 40 C4
Arnol 47 E1
Arnold 21 E2
Arnold 56 **C1**

Arnprior 38 A4
Arrochar 37 F4
Arundel 10 A4
Ascot 9 F1
Ascot 52 **A5**
Asfordby 21 E3
Ash *Kent* 53 **H5**
Ash *Surr.* 9 F1
Ashbourne 20 C2
Ashburton 5 D2
Ashbury 14 C4
Ashby de la Zouch 21 D3
Ashchurch 14 B2
Ashcott 7 F3
Ashford *Kent* 11 E2
Ashford *Surr.* 10 A1
Ashford *Surr.* 52 **B4**
Ashgill 61 **F3**
Ashington 31 D1
Ashkirk 34 C3
Ashley *Cambs.* 16 C3
Ashley *Ches.* 59 **E3**
Ashley Green 52 **A1**
Ashow 55 **F4**
Ashton 19 F2
Ashton 58 **C5**
Ashton-in-Makerfield 25 D4
Ashton-in-Makerfield 58 **C2**
Ashton-under-Lyne 25 E4
Ashton upon Mersey 59 **E2**
Ashurst 9 D3
Ashurst *E.Suss.* 10 C3
Ashurst *Hants.* 50 **A1**
Ashwick 8 A1
Askern 26 B3
Aspatria 29 E2
Aspull 59 **D1**
Astley *Warks.* 55 **F3**
Astley Green 59 **E2**
Aston *Ches.* 58 **C4**
Aston *Flint.* 58 **A5**
Aston *S.Yorks.* 57 **E4**
Aston *Staffs.* 56 **A4**
Aston *W.Mid.* 54 **C3**
Aston Clinton 15 F3
Aston Fields 54 **B4**
Aston on Trent 21 D2
Astwood Bank 14 C1
Astwood Bank 54 **C5**
Atherington 6 B4
Atherstone 20 C4
Atherstone 55 **F2**
Atherton 25 D4
Atherton 59 **D1**
Attadale 41 D3
Attenborough 56 **C2**
Attleborough *Norf.* 23 D4
Attleborough *Warks.* 55 **F2**

Attlebridge 23 E3
Auchallater 38 C1
Auchenblae 39 E1
Auchenbreck 33 D1
Auchencrow 35 E2
Auchindrain 37 E4
Auchinleck 33 F3
Auchinloch 61 E1
Auchmull 39 E1
Auchnagatt 43 F3
Aucholzie 39 D1
Auchterarder 38 B4
Auchtermuchty 39 D4
Auchtertool 34 B1
Audlem 20 A2
Audley 20 A2
Audley 56 A3
Aughton *Lancs.* 24 C4
Aughton *Lancs.* 58 A1
Aughton *S.Yorks.* 26 A4
Aughton *S.Yorks.* 57 E4
Aughton Park 58 B1
Auldearn 42 B2
Aultbea 41 D1
Aultguish Inn 41 E2
Aust 51 F3
Austrey 55 E1
Aveley 10 C1
Aveley 53 G3
Aviemore 42 B4
Avoch 42 A2
Avonbridge 34 A1
Avonmouth 7 F2
Avonmouth 51 F4
Awkley 51 F3
Awre 14 A3
Awsworth 21 D2
Awsworth 56 B1
Axminster 5 F1
Aycliffe 31 D3
Aylesbury 15 E3
Aylesford 11 D2
Aylesham 11 F2
Aylsham 23 E3
Ayr 33 E3
Aysgarth 30 C4

B

Babworth 26 B4
Backaland 49 E2
Backford 58 A4
Backwell 7 F2
Backworth 60 A1
Bacup 25 E3
Badcaul 44 A4
Baddeley Green 56 C3
Baddesley Ensor 55 E2
Badenscoth 43 E3
Badgerbank 59 F4
Badgers Mount 53 F5
Badlipster 45 F2
Badsey 14 B2
Bagh a' Chaisteil (Castlebay) 46 A4
Bagillt 19 E1
Baginton 55 F4
Baglan 6 C1
Bagnall 56 C3
Bagshot 9 F1
Baguley 59 F3
Baildon 25 F2
Baildon 57 D1
Baile a'Mhanaich 46 A2
Baile Ailein 47 E2
Baile Mhartainn 46 A1
Bainbridge 30 B4
Bainton 26 C2
Baker Street 53 H3

Bala 19 D3
Balbeggie 38 C3
Balblair 42 A2
Balcombe 10 B3
Baldernock 61 D1
Balderton 21 E2
Baldock 16 A2
Baldslow 11 D4
Baldwin's Gate 56 A4
Balemartine 36 A3
Balephuil 36 A3
Balfour 49 E3
Balfron 33 F1
Balgown 40 B2
Balgray 39 D3
Balintore 42 A2
Ballabeg 24 A3
Ballachulish 37 E2
Ballantrae 28 A1
Ballasalla 24 A3
Ballater 39 D1
Ballaugh 24 A2
Ball Haye Green 56 C3
Ballingry 38 C4
Ballinluig 38 C2
Ballintuim 38 C2
Balloch 33 E1
Ballochroy 32 C2
Ballygrant 32 A2
Balmacara 40 C3
Balmaha 33 E1
Balmedie 43 F4
Balmerlawn 50 A2
Balmore E.Dun. 61 E1
Balnacra 41 D3
Balnahard 36 C3
Balnapaling 42 A2
Balquhidder 38 A3
Balsall 55 E4
Balsall Common 55 E4
Baltasound 48 C1
Balterley 56 A3
Balvicar 37 D4
Bamburgh 35 F3
Bampton *Devon* 7 D4
Bampton *Oxon.* 14 C3
Banbury 15 D2
Banchory 39 E1
Banff 43 E2
Bangor 18 B1
Banham 23 D4
Bankfoot 38 C3
Bannockburn 34 A1
Banstead 10 B2
Banwell 7 F3
Barabhas 47 E1
Barassie 33 E3
Barbaraville 42 A2
Barby 15 D1
Bardney 22 A1
Bardsea 24 C1
Bargoed 7 E2
Bargrennan 28 B1
Barham 11 F2
Bar Hill 16 B1
Barking Gt.Lon. 53 F3
Barkingside 53 F3
Barkston 21 F2
Barkway 16 B2
Barlaston 20 B2
Barlborough 21 D1
Barley 16 B2
Barmouth 12 C1
Barmpton 60 A5
Barnacle 55 F3
Barnard Castle 30 C3
Barnes 52 D4
Barnet 52 D2
Barningham 17 D1
Barnoldswick 25 E2
Barnsley 26 A4

Barnstaple 6 C4
Barnt Green 54 C4
Barnton 20 A1
Barnton 59 D4
Barr 33 E3
Barrapol 36 A3
Barrhead 33 F2
Barrhead 61 D3
Barrhill 28 B1
Barrock 45 F1
Barrow-in-Furness 24 B1
Barrowford 25 E2
Barrow Nook 58 B1
Barrow upon Humber 27 D3
Barrow upon Soar 21 E3
Barry 7 E2
Barston 55 E4
Barthomley 56 A3
Bartley 50 A1
Barton (Preston) *Lancs.* 25 D2
Barton (Southport) Lancs. 58 A1
Barton-le-Clay 16 A3
Barton-under-Needwood 20 C3
Barton-upon-Humber 27 D3
Barton in Fabis 56 C2
Barton in the Beans 55 F1
Barwick in Elmet 57 F1
Baschurch 19 F3
Basford Green 56 C3
Basildon 11 D1
Basingstoke 9 E1
Baslow 20 C1
Bassaleg 51 E1
Bassett 50 B1
Bassingham 21 F1
Batchworth 52 B2
Batchworth Heath 52 B2
Bate Heath 59 D4
Bath 8 B1
Batheaston 8 B1
Bathford 8 B1
Bathgate 34 A1
Batley 25 F3
Batley 57 E2
Battersea 52 D4
Battle 11 D4
Bawdeswell 23 D3
Bawdsey 17 E2
Bawtry 26 B4
Baxterley 55 E2
Baycliff 24 C1
Bayford Herts. 53 E1
Bayston Hill 13 F1
Beaconsfield 10 A1
Beaconsfield 52 A2
Beadnell 35 F3
Beaminster 5 F1
Beamish 60 A3
Bean 53 G4
Bearsden 33 F1
Bearsden 61 D1
Bearsted 11 D2
Beattock 34 B4
Beauchamp Roding 53 G1
Beauchief 57 D4
Beaudesert 55 D5
Beaulieu 50 A2
Beauly 41 F3
Beaumaris 18 B1
Beausale 55 E4
Bebington 19 E1
Bebington 58 A3
Beccles 23 F4
Beckenham 53 E5
Beckingham 26 C4
Beckton 53 F3
Becontree 53 F3
Bedale 31 D4
Beddau 7 D2

Beddgelert 18 B2
Beddingham 10 C4
Beddington 53 E5
Beddington Corner 52 D5
Bedford 15 F2
Bedhampton 50 B4
Bedlington 30 C1
Bedmond 52 C1
Bedwas 7 E2
Bedwas 51 D1
Bedworth 21 D4
Bedworth 55 F3
Beeford 27 D2
Beer 5 E1
Beeston *Notts.* 21 D2
Beeston *Notts.* 56 C2
Beeston *W.Yorks.* 57 E1
Began 51 E1
Beighton *S.Yorks.* 26 A4
Beighton *S.Yorks.* 57 E4
Beith 33 E2
Belbroughton 20 B4
Belbroughton 54 B4
Belford 35 F3
Bell Bar 52 D1
Bell End 54 B4
Bellingdon 52 A1
Bellingham 30 B1
Bellshill *N.Lan.* 33 F2
Bellshill N.Lan. 61 F3
Belmont Gt.Lon. 52 D5
Belmont Shet. 48 C1
Belper 21 D2
Belper 56 A1
Belper Lane End 56 A1
Belsay 30 C1
Belvedere 53 F4
Bembridge 9 E4
Bempton 27 D1
Benenden 11 D3
Benllech 18 B1
Benson 15 E4
Bentley *S.Yorks.* 26 B4
Bentley Warks. 55 E2
Bentley Heath 55 D4
Benton Square 60 B1
Beoley 54 C5
Bepton 50 C3
Bere Alston 4 B2
Bere Ferrers 4 B2
Bere Regis 8 B3
Berinsfield 15 D4
Berkeley 14 A3
Berkhamsted 15 F3
Berkhamsted 52 A1
Berkswell 20 C4
Berkswell 55 E4
Bermondsey 53 E4
Berners Roding 53 H1
Bernisdale 40 B3
Berriedale 45 E3
Berrow 7 E3
Bersham 19 E2
Berwick-upon-Tweed 35 E2
Bessacarr 26 B4
Bethersden 11 E3
Bethesda 18 B2
Bethnal Green 53 E3
Betley 56 A4
Betsham 53 H4
Bettyhill 44 C1
Betws-y-coed 18 C2
Beverley 27 D2
Bewdley 20 A4
Bexhill 11 D4
Bexley 53 F4
Bexleyheath 53 F4
Bibury 14 C3
Bicester 15 E3
Bickenhill 55 D3
Bickerstaffe 58 B1

Bickleigh (Plymouth) *Devon* 4 C2
Bickleigh (Tiverton) *Devon* 5 D1
Bickley 53 F5
Bicknacre 11 D1
Biddenden 11 D3
Biddulph 56 B1
Biddulph Moor 56 B1
Bideford 6 B4
Bidford-on-Avon 14 C1
Bierley W.Yorks. 57 D1
Bigbury-on-Sea 4 C3
Biggar 34 A3
Biggin Hill 10 C2
Biggleswade 16 A2
Bilborough 56 C1
Bilbrook Staffs. 54 A1
Bilsber 45 F2
Billericay 16 C4
Billinge 25 D4
Billinge 58 C1
Billingham 31 D3
Billingham 60 B4
Billinghay 22 A2
Billingshurst 10 A3
Billockby 23 F3
Billy Row 30 C2
Bilston *Midloth.* 34 B2
Bilston W.Mid. 54 B2
Bilstone 55 F1
Bilton 27 D3
Bimbister 49 E3
Binbrook 27 D4
Binfield 9 F1
Bingham 21 E2
Bingley 25 F2
Bingley 57 D1
Binley W.Mid. 55 F4
Birch *Gt.Man.* 59 F1
Birchgrove Cardiff 51 D1
Birchgrove *N. & P.T.* 6 C1
Birchington 11 F1
Bircotes 26 B4
Bird End 54 C2
Birkenhead 19 E1
Birkenhead 58 A3
Birkenshaw 57 E2
Birley Carr 57 D3
Birmingham 20 C4
Birmingham 54 C3
Birmingham Airport 20 C4
Birmingham Airport 55 D3
Birsay 49 D2
Birstall 21 E3
Birstall Smithies 57 E2
Birtley *T. & W.* 31 D2
Birtley T. & W. 60 A3
Bishop's Castle 13 F2
Bishop's Cleeve 14 B2
Bishop's Hull 7 E4
Bishop's Itchington 15 D1
Bishop's Lydeard 7 E4
Bishop's Stortford 16 B3
Bishop's Tawton 6 C4
Bishop's Waltham 9 E3
Bishop's Waltham 50 C1
Bishop's Wood 54 A1
Bishop Auckland 30 C3
Bishopbriggs 33 F1
Bishopbriggs 61 E2
Bishopstoke 50 B1
Bishopston 6 C2
Bishopton Dur. 60 A4
Bishopton *Renf.* 33 F1
Bishton 51 D3
Bisley 14 B3
Bitterne 50 B1
Bitton 8 A1
Bixter 48 B3

Blaby 21 D4
Black Bourton 14 C3
Blackburn *Aber.* 43 E4
Blackburn *Lancs.* 25 D3
Blackburn *W.Loth.* 34 A2
Blackden Heath 59 E4
Blackfield 50 B2
Blackford 38 B4
Blackhall 61 E4
Blackhall Colliery 31 D2
Blackheath *W.Mid.* 54 B3
Blacklunans 38 C2
Blackmoor Gate 6 C3
Blackmore 53 H1
Black Notley 16 C3
Blackpool 24 C2
Blackpool Airport 24 C3
Blackridge 34 A1
Blacktown 51 E1
Blackwaterfoot 32 C3
Blackwell *H. & W.* 54 B4
Blackwood 7 E1
Blackwood Hill 56 C3
Blacon 58 A5
Blaenau Ffestiniog 18 C2
Blaenavon 7 E1
Blaengarw 7 D1
Blaengwrach 7 D1
Blagdon 7 F3
Blaich 37 E1
Blaina 7 E1
Blair Atholl 38 B2
Blairgowrie 38 C3
Blakebrook 54 A4
Blakedown 54 A4
Blakelaw *T. & W.* 60 A2
Blakeney *Glos.* 14 A3
Blakeney *Norf.* 23 D2
Blakenhall *Ches.* 56 A4
Blakenhall *W.Mid.* 54 B2
Blakeshall 54 A3
Blandford Forum 8 B3
Blaydon 30 C1
Blean 11 E2
Blendworth 50 B3
Bletchley 15 F2
Blewbury 15 D4
Blisworth 15 E1
Blockley 14 C2
Blossomfield 55 D4
Bloxham 15 D2
Bloxwich 54 B1
Blubberhouses 25 F2
Blyth *Nhumb.* 31 D1
Blyth *Notts.* 26 B4
Blyth Bridge 34 B2
Blythe Bridge 56 C4
Blythe Marsh 56 C4
Blyton 26 C4
Bo'ness 34 A1
Boarhunt 50 A4
Boath 41 F2
Boat of Garten 42 B4
Bobbington 54 A2
Bobbingworth 53 G1
Boddam *Aber.* 43 F3
Boddam *Shet.* 48 B4
Bodelwyddan 19 D1
Bodenham 13 F3
Bodicote 15 D2
Bodmin 4 A2
Bogniebrae 43 D3
Bognor Regis 9 F3
Bold Heath 58 C3
Boldon 31 D2
Boldon 60 B2
Boldre 9 D3
Bollington (Altrincham)
  ***Ches.* 59 E3**
Bollington (Macclesfield)
  Ches. 20 B1

Bolnhurst 16 A1
Bolsover 21 D1
Boltby 31 D4
Bolton *E.Loth.* 34 C1
Bolton *Gt.Man.* 25 D3
Bolton *Gt.Man.* 59 E1
Bolton-le-Sands 24 C1
Bolventor 4 A2
Bonar Bridge 44 C4
Bonawe Quarries 37 E3
Bonchester Bridge 35 D4
Bonehill 55 D1
Bonhill 33 E1
Boningale 54 A1
Bonjedward 35 D3
Bonnybridge 34 A1
Bonnyrigg 34 C2
Bonvilston 7 E2
Boothstown 59 E1
Bootle *Cumb.* 29 E4
Bootle *Mers.* 19 E1
Bootle *Mers.* 58 A2
Boreham 16 C3
Borehamwood 16 A4
Borehamwood 52 C2
Boreland 34 B4
Boreraig 40 A2
Borgh 46 A4
Borgue *D. & G.* 28 C2
Borgue *High.* 45 E3
Boroughbridge 26 A1
Borough Green 10 C2
Borrowash 21 D3
Borrowash 56 B2
Borrowdale 29 F3
Borth 12 C3
Borve 40 B3
Bosbury 14 A2
Boscastle 4 A1
Bosham 9 F3
Bosham 50 C4
Bostock Green 59 D5
Boston 22 A2
Boston Spa 26 A2
Botany Bay 52 D2
Botesdale 17 D1
Bothel 29 E2
Bothenhampton 5 F1
Bothwell 61 F3
Botley *Bucks.* 52 A1
Botley *Hants.* 50 C1
Bottesford *Leics.* 21 E2
Bottesford *N.Lincs.* 26 C3
Boughton 21 E1
Bournbrook 54 C3
Bourne 22 A3
Bournebridge 53 G2
Bourne End *Bucks.* 15 F4
Bourne End *Herts.* 52 B1
Bournemouth 8 B3
Bournemouth (Hurn) Airport
  8 C4
Bournheath 54 B4
Bournmoor 31 D2
Bournmoor 60 B3
Bournville 54 C3
Bourton 8 B2
Bourton-on-the-Water 14 C3
Boveney 52 A4
Bovey Tracey 5 D2
Bovingdon 52 B1
Bovinger 53 G1
Bow 49 E4
Bowburn 31 D2
Bowdon 59 E3
Bowes 30 B3
Bowmore 32 A2
Bowness-on-Solway 29 E1
Bowness-on-Windermere
  29 F4
Box 8 B1

Boxmoor 52 B1
Boyton Cross 53 H1
Bozeat 15 F1
Braaid 24 A3
Bracadale 40 A3
Bracebridge Heath 21 F1
Brackley 15 E2
Bracknell 9 F1
Braco 38 B4
Bracora 37 D1
Bradbury 60 A4
Bradford *W.Yorks.* 25 F2
Bradford *W.Yorks.* 57 D1
Bradford-on-Avon 8 B1
Brading 9 E4
Bradley *W.Mid.* 54 B2
Bradmore *Notts.* 56 C2
Bradmore *W.Mid.* 54 A2
Bradninch 5 E1
Bradpole 5 F1
Bradshaw 25 D3
Bradwall Green 59 E5
Bradwell *Derbys.* 25 F4
Bradwell *Norf.* 23 F4
Bradwell Waterside 17 D3
Brae 48 B2
Braeantra 41 F1
Braemar 38 C1
Bragar 47 E1
Brailsford 20 C2
Braintree 16 C3
Braithwaite 29 E3
Braithwell 26 B4
Braithwell 57 F3
Bramcote 56 C2
Bramford 17 E2
Bramhall 25 E4
Bramhall 59 F3
Bramley *S.Yorks.* 26 A4
Bramley *S.Yorks.* 57 E3
Brampton *Cambs.* 16 A1
Brampton *Cumb.* 30 A2
Brampton *Suff.* 17 F1
**Brampton-en-le-Morthen
  57 E4**
Brancaster 22 C2
Brandesburton 27 D2
Brandon *Dur.* 30 C2
Brandon *Suff.* 22 C4
Branson's Cross 54 C4
Branston 21 F1
Brantham 17 E2
Bratton 8 B1
Braunston 15 D1
Braunstone 21 D3
Braunton 6 B4
Bray 10 A1
Brayton 26 B3
Breadsall 56 A2
Breage 3 E3
Breakish 40 C4
Bream 14 A3
Breanais 47 D2
Breascleit 47 E2
Breaston 21 D2
Breaston 56 B2
Brechfa 12 B4
Brechin 39 E2
Brecon 13 D4
Bredbury 25 E4
Bredon 14 B2
Brenkley 60 A1
Brent 52 C3
Brentford 52 C4
Brentwood 10 C1
Brentwood 53 G2
Brereton Green 59 E5
Brereton Heath 59 F5
Bretton 19 E2
Bretton 58 A5
Brewood 20 B3

Brewood 54 A1
Bricket Wood 52 C1
Bridge 11 E2
Bridgemary 50 C2
Bridgemere 56 A4
Bridgend *Angus* 39 E2
Bridgend *Bridg.* 7 D2
Bridgend *Moray* 42 C3
Bridgend (Islay) *Arg. & B.*
  32 A2
Bridgend (Lochgilphead)
  Arg. & B. 32 C1
Bridge of Allan 38 B4
Bridge of Balgie 38 A2
Bridge of Cally 38 C2
Bridge of Craigisla 39 D2
Bridge of Don 43 F4
Bridge of Dun 39 E2
Bridge of Dye 39 E1
Bridge of Earn 38 C4
Bridge of Orchy 37 F3
Bridge of Walls 48 B3
Bridge of Weir 33 E2
Bridge Trafford 58 B4
Bridgnorth 20 A4
Bridgtown 54 B1
Bridgwater 7 F4
Bridlington 27 D1
Bridport 5 F1
Brierfield 25 E2
Brierley Hill 54 B3
Brierton 60 B4
Brigg 26 C3
Brigham 29 E3
Brighouse 25 F3
Brighouse 57 D2
Brighstone 9 D4
Brightlingsea 17 D3
Brighton 10 B4
Brightons 34 A1
Brig o'Turk 38 A4
Brigstock 21 F4
Brimington 21 D1
Brimstage 58 A3
Brindley Ford 56 B3
Brinian 49 E2
Brinsley 21 D2
Brinsley 56 B1
Brinsworth 26 A4
Brinsworth 57 E4
Bristol 14 A4
Bristol 51 F4
Bristol (Lulsgate) Airport 7 F2
Briston 23 D3
Briton Ferry 6 C1
Brixham 5 D3
Brixworth 15 E1
Broadbridge 50 C4
Broad Clyst 5 D1
Broadford 40 C4
Broad Haven 12 A2
Broad Heath 14 A1
Broadheath 59 E3
Broadley Common 53 F1
Broadmayne 8 B4
Broad Oak 11 D3
Broadstairs 11 F2
Broadstreet Common 51 D3
Broadway 14 C2
Broadwey 8 A4
Broadwindsor 5 F1
Brochel 40 B3
Brockbridge 50 A3
Brockenhurst 9 D3
Brockenhurst 50 A2
Brockworth 14 B3
Brodick 33 D3
**Broken Cross (Macclesfield)
  Ches. 59 F4**
**Broken Cross (Northwich)
  Ches. 59 D4**

Bromborough 58 A3
Bromham *Beds.* 15 F1
Bromham *Wilts.* 8 C1
Bromley 53 F5
Brompton 31 D4
Brompton on Swale 30 C4
Bromsgrove 14 B1
Bromsgrove 54 B4
Bromyard 14 A1
Bronaber 18 C3
Brooke 23 E4
Brookmans Park 16 A4
Brookmans Park 52 D1
Brook Street *Essex* 53 G2
Broome *H. & W.* 54 B4
Broomedge 59 E3
Broomfield 16 C3
Brora 45 D4
Broseley 20 A4
Brotton 31 E3
Brough *Cumb.* 30 B3
Brough *E.Riding* 26 C3
Brough *High.* 45 E1
Brough *Shet.* 48 C2
Broughton *Bord.* 34 B3
Broughton *Flint.* 19 E3
Broughton *Flint.* 58 A5
Broughton *Gt.Man.* 59 F2
Broughton *N.Lincs.* 26 C3
Broughton *Nhants.* 21 F4
Broughton Astley 21 D4
Broughton in Furness 29 E4
Broughtown 49 F2
Broughty Ferry 39 E3
Brown Edge *Staffs.* 56 C3
Brownhills *W.Mid.* 20 B3
Brownhills *W.Mid.* 54 C1
Brown Lees 56 B3
Brownshill Green 55 F3
Broxbourne 53 E1
Broxburn 34 B1
Brundall 23 E3
Brundish 17 F1
Bruton 8 A2
Bryn *Gt.Man.* 58 C1
Brynamman 6 C1
Brynford 19 E1
Bryn Gates 58 C1
Brynmawr 7 E1
Bubbenhall 55 F4
Bubwith 26 B2
Buchlyvie 33 F1
Buckden *Cambs.* 16 A1
Buckden *N.Yorks.* 25 E1
Buckfastleigh 4 C2
Buckhaven 39 D4
Buckhurst Hill 53 F2
Buckie 43 D2
Buckingham 15 E2
Buckland Common 52 A1
Bucklebury 9 E1
Bucklers Hard 50 B2
Buckley 19 E2
Bucknall *Staffs.* 56 C4
Bucksburn 43 E4
Bucks Hill 52 B1
Budbrooke 55 E5
Bude 4 A1
Budleigh Salterton 5 E2
Bugbrooke 15 E1
Builth Wells 13 D3
Buldoo 45 E1
Bulford 8 C2
Bulkington *Warks.* 21 D4
Bulkington *Warks.* 55 F3
Bulmer Tye 17 D2
Bulphan 53 H3
Bulwell 56 C1
Bumble's Green 53 F1
Bunessan 36 B3
Bungay 23 E4

Buntingford 16 B3
Burbage 9 D1
Bures 17 D2
Burford 14 C3
Burgess Hill 10 B3
Burgh by Sands 29 F2
Burghead 42 B2
Burghfield Common 9 E1
Burghill 13 F3
Burgh le Marsh 22 B1
Burley 9 D3
Burley in Wharfdale 25 F2
Burnage 59 F2
Burness 49 F2
Burnham *Bucks.* 10 A1
Burnham *Bucks.* 52 A3
Burnham-on-Crouch 17 D4
Burnham-on-Sea 7 E3
Burnham Market 22 C2
Burnhouse 33 E2
Burniston 31 F4
Burnley 25 E2
Burnmouth 35 E2
Burnopfield 30 C2
Burntisland 34 B1
Burntwood 20 C3
Burntwood Green 20 C3
Burntwood Green 54 C1
Burradon *T. & W.* 60 A1
Burravoe 48 C2
Burrelton 38 C3
Burridge 50 C1
Burrowhill 52 A5
Burry Port 6 B1
Burscough 24 C3
Burscough Bridge 24 C3
Bursledon 9 E3
Bursledon 50 B2
Burslem 56 B4
**Burton (Delamere) *Ches.*
58 C5**
Burton (Wirral) *Ches.* 58 A4
Burton-in-Kendal 25 D1
Burton Bradstock 5 F1
Burton Green *Warks.* 55 E4
Burton Joyce 21 E2
Burton Latimer 15 F1
Burton Leonard 26 A1
Burton upon Stather 26 C3
Burton upon Trent 20 C3
Burtonwood 58 C2
Burwardsley 19 F2
Burwarton 20 A4
Burwash 11 D3
Burwell 16 B1
Burwick 49 E4
Bury 25 E3
Bury St. Edmunds 17 D1
Busby *E.Renf.* 61 D3
Bushbury 54 B1
Bushey 16 A4
Bushey 52 C2
Bushey Heath 52 C2
Butler's Hill 56 C1
Buttermere 29 E3
Butters Green 56 B3
Buttershaw 57 D2
Butterwick 26 C1
Butt Lane 56 B3
Buxted 10 C3
Buxton 20 B1
Byfield 15 D1
Byfleet 10 A2
Byfleet 52 B5
Byker 60 A2
Bylchau 19 D2
Byley 59 E5

C

Cadder 61 E1
Cadishead 59 E2

Cadnam 50 A1
Caerau *Cardiff* 7 E2
Caerau *Cardiff* 51 D2
Caergwrle 19 E2
Caerhun 18 C1
Caerleon 7 F1
Caernarfon 18 B2
Caerphilly 7 E2
Caerphilly 51 D1
Caerwent 7 F1
Cairnbaan 32 C1
Cairneyhill 34 A1
Cairnryan 28 A1
Caister-on-Sea 23 F3
Caistor 27 D4
Calanais 47 E2
Caldbeck 29 F2
Caldecote *Warks.* 55 F2
Caldecott 21 F4
Calderbank 61 F2
Caldercruix 34 A1
Calderglen 61 E3
Caldicot 7 F2
Caldicot 51 E3
Caldwell 30 C3
Calfsound 49 E2
Calgary 36 B2
Callander 38 A4
Callington 4 B2
Calmore 50 A1
Calne 14 B4
Calshot 50 B2
Calver 20 C1
Calverley 57 E1
Calverton 21 E2
Calvine 38 B2
Cam 14 A3
Camasnacroise 37 D2
Camberley 9 F1
Camberwell 53 E4
Camborne 3 E3
Cambridge 16 B2
Cambridge Airport 16 B2
Cambuslang 61 E2
Camden 52 D3
Camelford 4 A2
Camer 53 H5
Campbeltown 32 C3
Camperdown 60 A1
Camptown 35 D4
Camrose 12 A1
Cannich 41 E3
Cannington 7 E3
Cannock 20 B3
Canonbie 29 F1
Canterbury 11 E2
Canton 7 E2
Canton 51 D2
Canvey Island 11 D1
Caolas 36 A2
Caolas Scalpaigh 47 E3
Capel 10 B3
Capel Curig 18 C2
Capel St. Mary 17 D2
Capenhurst 58 A4
Cappercleuch 34 B3
Capplegill 34 B4
Caputh 38 C3
Carbost (Loch Harport) 40 B3
Carbost (Loch Snizort Beag)
40 B3
Carcroft 26 B3
Cardenden 39 D4
Cardiff 7 E2
Cardiff 51 D2
Cardiff Wales Airport 7 D2
Cardigan 12 A3
Cardross 33 E1
Cargenbridge 29 D1

Cargill 38 C3
Cargo Fleet 60 C4
Carlabhagh 47 E1
Carlisle 29 F2
Carlops 34 B2
Carlton *Leics.* 55 F1
Carlton *Notts.* 21 E2
Carlton *Stock.* 60 A4
Carlton *W.Yorks.* 57 F2
Carlton-on-Trent 21 E1
Carlton Colville 23 F4
Carlton in Lindrick 26 B4
Carlton in Lindrick 57 F4
Carluke 34 A2
Carmarthen 12 B4
Carmunnock 61 E3
Carmyle 61 E2
Carmyllie 39 E3
Carnbee 39 E4
Carnbo 38 C4
Carnforth 24 C1
Carno 13 D1
Carnoustie 39 E3
Carnwath 34 A2
Carradale 32 C3
Carrbridge 42 B4
Carrington *Gt.Man.* 59 E2
Carronbridge 34 A4
Carsaig 36 C3
Carshalton 52 D5
Carsluith 28 C2
Carsphairn 33 F4
Carstairs 34 A2
Carterton 14 C3
Cartmel 24 C1
Castle Bromwich 20 C4
Castle Bromwich 55 D3
Castle Carrock 30 A2
Castle Cary 8 A2
Castle Donnington 21 D3
Castle Douglas 29 D2
Castle End 55 E4
Castleford 26 A3
Castle Kennedy 28 A2
Castlemartin 12 A2
Castlemilk 61 E3
Castleside 30 C2
Castleton *Newport* 51 E1
Castleton *N.Yorks.* 31 E4
Castletown *High.* 45 E1
Castletown *I.o.M.* 24 A3
Castletown *T. & W.* 60 B3
Catbrain 51 F3
Catcliffe 57 E4
Caterham 10 B2
Catford 53 E4
Catherington 50 A3
Caton 25 D1
Catrine 33 F3
Catshill 14 B1
Catterick 30 C4
Catterick Camp 30 C4
Caunsall 54 A3
Caverswall 20 B2
Caverswall 56 C4
Cawdor 42 A2
Cawood 26 B2
Cawston 23 E3
Caythorpe 21 F2
Cayton 27 D1
Ceann a'Bhàigh 46 A1
Cearsiadar 47 E2
Cefn-mawr 19 E2
Cellarhead 56 C4
Ceres 39 D4
Cerrigydrudion 19 D2
Chadderton 25 E4
Chaddesden 56 A2
Chaddesley Corbett 54 A4
Chad Valley 54 C3

Chadwell St. Mary 53 H4
Chadwick End 55 E4
Chagford 4 C1
Chailey 10 B3
Chalfont Common 52 B2
Chalfont St. Giles 10 A1
Chalfont St. Giles 52 A2
Chalfont St. Peter 52 B2
Chalford 14 B3
Chalgrove 15 E4
Chalk 53 H4
Chalton *Hants.* 50 B3
Champany 34 A1
Chandler's Cross 52 B2
Chapel-en-le-Frith 25 F4
**Chapel Allerton *W.Yorks.*
57 F1**
Chapel End 55 F2
Chapel Fields 55 F4
Chapelhall 34 A2
Chapelhall 61 F2
Chapel St. Leonards 22 B1
Chapeltown *S.Yorks.* 26 A4
Chapeltown *S.Yorks.* 57 D3
Chard 5 F1
Chardstock 5 F1
Charfield 14 A4
Charing 11 E2
Charlbury 15 D3
Charlestown 43 F4
Charlestown of Aberlour
42 C3
Charlesworth 25 E4
Charlton *Gt.Lon.* 53 F4
Charlton *Hants.* 9 D1
Charlton *W.Suss.* 50 B3
Charlton *Wilts.* 14 B4
Charlton Kings 14 B3
Charlwood 10 B3
Charminster 8 A3
Charmouth 5 F1
Chartham 11 E2
Chartridge 52 A1
Chasetown 54 C1
Chatham 11 D2
Chatteris 22 B4
Chatton 35 E3
Cheadle *Gt.Man.* 25 E4
Cheadle *Gt.Man.* 59 F3
Cheadle *Staffs.* 20 B2
Cheadle Hulme 59 F3
Cheam 52 D5
Cheapside 52 A5
Checkley *Ches.* 56 A4
Checkley *Staffs.* 20 B2
Chedburgh 16 C2
Cheddar 7 F3
Cheddleton 20 B2
Cheddleton 56 C3
Cheetham Hill 59 F1
Chelford 59 F4
Chellaston 56 A2
Chelmorton 20 C1
Chelmsford 16 C3
Cheltenham 14 B3
Chenies 52 B2
Chepstow 7 F1
Cheriton 9 E2
Chertsey 10 A2
Chertsey 52 B5
Chesham 15 F3
Chesham Bois 52 A2
Cheshunt 16 B4
Cheshunt 53 E1
Cheslyn Hay 54 B1
Chessington 52 C5
Chester 19 F2
Chester 58 B5
Chester-le-Street 31 D2

Chester-le-Street 60 A3
Chesterfield *Derbys.* 21 D1
Chesterfield *Staffs.* 55 D1
Chesters 35 D4
Chesterton *Staffs.* 56 B4
Chew Magna 8 A1
Chichester 9 F3
Chichester 50 C4
Chickerell 8 A4
Chidden 50 A3
Chiddingfold 9 F2
Chidham 50 B4
Chieveley 15 D4
Chignall St. James 53 H1
Chigwell 10 C1
Chigwell 53 F2
Chigwell Row 53 F2
Chilcompton 8 A1
Childerditch 53 H3
Childer Thornton 58 A4
Childrey 15 D4
Childwall 58 B3
Chilgrove 50 C3
Chilham 11 E2
Chilton 3 D3
Chilvers Coton 55 F2
Chilworth *Hants.* 50 B1
Chingford 10 B1
Chingford 53 E2
Chinnor 15 E3
Chippenham 14 B4
Chipperfield 52 B1
Chipping Campden 14 C2
Chipping Norton 14 C2
Chipping Ongar 16 B4
Chipping Ongar 53 G1
Chipping Sodbury 14 A4
Chirbury 13 E1
Chirk 19 E3
Chirnside 35 E2
Chiseldon 14 C4
Chislehurst 53 F4
Chiswell Green 52 C1
Chiswick 53 D4
Chobham 52 A5
Cholesbury 52 A1
Chopwell 30 C2
Chorley 25 D3
Chorleywood 15 F4
Chorleywood 52 B2
Chorlton 56 A3
Chorlton-cum-Hardy 59 F2
Christchurch *Dorset* 8 C4
Christchurch *Newport* 51 D3
Christleton 58 B5
Christon Bank 35 F3
Chryston 33 F1
Chryston 61 E1
Chudleigh 5 D2
Chulmleigh 6 C4
Church Aston 20 A3
Churchdown 14 B3
Church End *Warks.* 55 E2
Churchgate 53 E1
Churchill *H. & W.* 54 A4
Church Lawton 20 B1
Church Lawton 56 B3
Church Stretton 13 F1
Churwell 57 E2
Cilcain 19 E2
Cille Bhrighde 46 A3
Cinderford 14 A3
Cirencester 14 B3
City of London 53 E3
City of Westminster 52 D3
Clabhach 36 A2
Clachan (Kintyre) *Arg. & B.*
32 C2
Clachan (Loch Fyne) *Arg. & B.*
37 E4
Clachan (Raasay) *High.* 40 B3

Clachan of Glendaruel 33 D1
Clachtoll 44 A3
Clackmannan 34 A1
Clacton-on-Sea 17 E3
Cladich 37 E3
Claggan 37 D2
Clanfield *Hants.* **50 B3**
Clanfield *Oxon.* 14 C3
Claonaig 32 C2
Clapham *Beds.* 15 F1
Clapham *Gt.Lon.* **52 D4**
Clapham *N.Yorks.* 25 D1
Clapton-in-Gordano **51 E4**
Clarborough 26 B4
Clare 16 C2
Clarkston 61 D3
Clashmore 42 A1
Clashnessie 44 A3
Clatterford End 53 G1
Claverdon 55 D5
Clavering 16 B3
Clay Cross 21 D1
Claydon 17 E2
Claygate *Surr.* **52 C5**
Clayhanger *W.Mid.* **54 C1**
Claypole 21 F2
Clayton *Staffs.* **56 B4**
Clayton *W.Suss.* 10 B4
Clayton *W.Yorks.* **57 D1**
Clayton-le-Moors 25 D3
Clayton-le-Woods 25 D3
Clayton West 25 F3
Cleadale 36 C1
Cleadon 31 D1
Cleadon 60 B2
Cleat 49 E4
Cleator Moor 29 E3
Cleckheaton 25 F3
Cleckheaton 57 D2
Cleehill 14 A1
Cleethorpes 27 E3
Clehonger 13 F4
Cleland 34 A2
Cleland 61 F3
Clenchwarton 22 B3
Clent 20 B4
Clent 54 B4
Cleobury Mortimer 14 A1
Clestrain 49 D3
Clevedon 7 F2
Clevedon 51 E4
Cleveleys 24 C2
Clewer Village 52 A4
Cliffe 11 D1
Cliffe Woods 11 D1
Clifton *Bristol* **51 F4**
Clifton *Notts.* **56 C2**
Clipstone 21 E1
Clitheroe 25 D2
Clock Face 58 C2
Closeburn 34 A4
Clotton 58 C5
Cloughton 31 F4
Clova 39 D1
Clovelly 6 B4
Clovenfords 34 C3
Clovullin 37 E2
Clowne 21 D1
Clun 13 E2
Clunes 37 E1
Clutton 8 A1
Clydach 6 C1
Clydebank 33 F1
Clydebank 61 D2
Clynderwen 12 A4
Clyro 13 E3
Coalburn 34 A3
Coalpit Hill 56 B3
Coalville 21 D3
Coast 41 D1
Coatbridge 33 F2

Coatbridge 61 F2
Coatham 60 C4
Coatham *Surr.* 10 A2
Cock Bridge 42 C4
Cockburnspath 35 D1
Cockenzie & Port Seton 34 C1
Cockerham 24 C2
Cockermouth 29 E3
Cockett 6 C1
Cockfield 30 C3
Cockfosters 52 D2
Cocking 50 C3
Coddenham 17 E2
Coddington 21 F1
Codicote 16 A3
Codnor 21 D2
Codnor 56 B1
Codsall 20 B3
Codsall 54 A1
Codsall Wood 54 A1
Coedkernew 51 E1
Cofton Hackett 54 C4
Cogan 51 D2
Coggeshall 17 D3
Colbury 50 A1
Colchester 17 D3
Coldblow 53 G4
Colden Common 9 E2
Coldingham 35 E2
Coldstream 35 E3
Coleford 14 A3
Colehill 8 C3
Coleshill *Bucks.* **52 A2**
Coleshill *Warks.* 20 C4
Coleshill *Warks.* **55 E3**
Colintraive 33 D1
Collafirth 48 B2
Collier Row 53 G2
Colliery Row 60 B3
Collieston 43 F3
Collin 29 E1
Collingham 21 F1
Collins Green 58 C2
Collycroft 55 F3
Colmonell 28 A1
Colnabaichin 42 C4
Colnbrook 10 A1
Colnbrook 52 B4
Colne 25 E2
Colney Heath 16 A4
Colney Heath 52 D1
Colney Street 52 C1
Colquhar 34 C2
Colsterworth 21 F3
Coltishall 20 D3
Colwich 20 B3
Colwick 21 E2
Colwyn Bay 18 C1
Colyford 5 E1
Colyton 5 E1
Combe Martin 6 C3
Comberbach 59 D4
Comberford 55 D2
Comberton 16 B2
Combe St. Nicholas 7 E4
Compton *W.Suss.* **50 B3**
Comrie 38 B3
Condorrat 61 F1
Congdon's Shop 4 B2
Congerstone 55 F1
Congleton 20 B1
Congleton 59 F5
Congresbury 7 F2
Coningsby 22 A2
Conisbrough 26 A4
Conisbrough 57 F3
Coniston 29 F4
Connah's Quay 19 E1
Connel 37 D3

Conon Bridge 41 F2
Consall 56 C4
Consett 30 C2
Constantine 3 E3
Contin 41 F2
Conwy 18 C1
Cookham 15 F4
Cookley *H. & W.* 20 B4
Cookley *H. & W.* **54 A3**
Cookshill 56 C4
Cooksmill Green 53 H1
Coombe Bissett 8 C2
Cooper's Hill 52 A4
Coopersale Common 53 F1
Copley 30 C3
Coppenhall Moss 56 A3
Copplestone 5 D1
Coppull 25 D3
Copt Heath 55 D4
Copythorne 9 D3
Copythorne 50 A1
Corbridge 30 B1
Corby 21 F4
Corfe Castle 8 C4
Corfe Mullen 8 C3
Corley 55 E3
Corley Ash 55 E3
Corley Moor 55 E3
Cornhill 43 D2
Cornhill-on-Tweed 35 E3
Cornholme 25 E3
Corpach 37 E1
Corrie 33 D3
Corringham 11 D1
Corsham 8 B1
Corsock 29 D1
Corstorphine 61 D4
Corton 23 F4
Corwen 19 D2
Coryton 11 D1
Cosby 21 D4
Coseley 54 A4
Cosham 50 A4
Coshieville 38 B2
Cossall 56 B1
Cotebrook 58 C5
Cotgrave 21 E2
Coton *Staffs.* **55 D1**
Cottenham 16 B1
Cotteridge 55 C3
Cottesmore 21 F3
Cottingham *E.Riding* 27 D2
Cottingham *Nhants.* 21 F4
Coulby Newham 60 C5
Coulport 33 E1
Coundon 30 C3
Coupar *Angus* 39 D3
Court House Green 55 F3
Cove 40 C1
Cove Bay 43 F4
Coven 54 B1
Coventry 21 D4
Coventry 55 F4
Coventry Airport 55 F4
Coverack 3 F4
Cowbit 22 A3
Cowbridge 7 D2
Cowdenbeath 34 B1
Cowes 9 E4
Cowfold 10 B3
Cowie 34 A1
Cowley *Gt.Lon.* **52 B3**
Cowling 25 E2
Cowpen Bewley 60 B4
Cowplain 50 A3
Cowshill 30 B2
Coxbench 56 A1
Coxheath 11 D2
Coxtie Green 53 G2
Coxwold 26 B1
Coychurch 7 D2

Coylton 33 E3
Coylumbridge 42 B4
Crabbs Cross 54 C5
Cradley *H. & W.* 14 A2
Cradley *W.Mid.* **54 B3**
Craghead 60 A3
Craichie 39 D3
Craig 41 D3
Craigandaive 33 D1
Craigdarroch 33 F4
Craigellachie 42 C3
Craigendoran 33 E1
Craighat 33 F1
Craiglockhart 61 E4
Craignure 37 D3
Craigmillar 61 E4
Crail 39 E4
Cramlington 30 B1
Cramlington 60 A1
Cramond 34 B1
Cramond 61 D4
Cranage 20 B1
Cranage 59 E5
Cranborne 52 A4
Cranfield 15 F2
Cranford *Gt.Lon.* **52 C4**
Cranham *Gt.Lon.* **53 G3**
Crank 58 C1
Cranleigh 10 A3
Cranshaws 35 D2
Cranwell 21 F2
Crask Inn 44 C3
Craster 35 F3
Crathie 39 D1
Craven Arms 13 F2
Crawford *Lancs.* **58 B1**
Crawfordjohn 34 A3
Crawley 10 B3
Crayford 53 G4
Creag Ghoraidh 46 B2
Credenhill 13 F3
Crediton 5 D1
Creekmouth 53 F3
Creetown 28 C2
Cregneish 24 A3
Creswell 21 D1
Crewe 20 A1
Crewe 56 A3
Crewkerne 5 F1
Crewton 56 A2
Crianlarich 37 F3
Criccieth 18 B3
Crick 51 E3
Crickhowell 13 E4
Cricklade 14 C4
Crieff 38 B3
Crigglestone 26 A3
Crimond 43 F2
Crinan 37 D4
Cringleford 23 E4
Cripp's Corner 11 D3
Crockenhill 53 G5
Crocketford or Ninemile Bar 29 D1
Croeserw 7 D1
Croft *Ches.* **59 D2**
Crofton 26 A3
Crofty 6 B1
Cromarty 42 A2
Cromer 23 E2
Cromford 20 C1
Cromhall 14 A4
Crondall 9 F1
Cronton 58 B3
Crook 30 C3
Crookham 35 E3
Crosbost 47 E2
Crosby *Mers.* 24 C4
Crosby *Mers.* **58 A2**
Crosby *N.Lincs.* 26 C3
Crosby Ravensworth 30 A3

Crossaig 32 C2
Crosscanonby 29 E2
Crossford *Fife* 34 B1
Crossford *S.Lan.* 34 A2
Cross Gates 57 F1
Crossgates *Fife* 34 B1
Crossgates *Powys* 13 E3
Crosshands 33 F3
Crosshill 33 E4
Cross Hill 56 B1
Crosshouse 33 F3
Cross Inn 12 C3
Crossmichael 28 C1
Crossway 13 D3
Crossway Green 54 A5
Croston 24 C3
Croughton 15 D2
Crowborough 10 C3
Crow Hill 14 A2
Crowland 22 A3
Crowle 26 C3
Crowthorne 9 F1
Crowton 58 C4
Croxley Green 52 B2
Croy *High.* 42 A3
Croy *N.Lan.* 33 F1
Croy *N.Lan.* **61 F1**
Croyde 6 B3
Croydon *Gt.Lon.* **53 E5**
Cruden Bay 43 F3
Crulabhig 47 E2
Crumlin 7 E1
Crutherland 61 E3
Crymych 12 A4
Crynant 6 C1
Crystal Palace 53 E4
Cubbington 15 D1
Cubbington 55 F5
Cuckfield 10 B3
Cuddington *Ches.* 19 F1
Cuddington *Ches.* **59 D4**
Cudworth 26 A3
Cuffley 16 A4
Cuffley 53 E1
Culbokie 41 F2
Culcheth 19 F1
Culcheth 59 D2
Culdrain 43 D3
Cullen 43 D2
Cullercoats 60 B1
Cullicudden 42 A2
Cullingworth 25 F2
Cullipool 37 D4
Cullivoe 48 C1
Cullompton 5 E1
Culmstock 7 E4
Culnacraig 44 A4
Culnaknock 40 B2
Culross 34 A1
Culswick 48 B3
Cults 43 E4
Culverstone Green 53 H5
Cumbernauld 34 A1
Cumbernauld 61 F1
Cuminestown 43 E2
Cumnock 33 F3
Cumnor 15 D3
Cunningsburgh 48 B4
Cupar 39 D4
Curbridge *Hants.* **50 C1**
Curdridge 50 C1
Curdworth 55 D2
Curry Rivel 7 F4
Cutnall Green 54 A5
Cwm 7 E1
Cwmafan 6 C1
Cwmbran 7 E1
Cwmllynfell 6 C1
Cymmer 7 D1
Cynghordy 13 D4
Cynwyl Elfed 12 B4

D

Dacre 29 F3
Dagenham 53 F3
Dail Bho Thuath 47 F1
Dailly 33 E4
Dairsie 39 D4
Dalabrog 46 A3
Dalbeattie 29 D2
Dalby 24 A3
Dale *Derbys.* **56 B2**
Dale *Pembs.* 12 A2
Dalgety Bay 34 B1
Dalham 16 C1
Dalkeith 34 C2
Dallas 42 B2
Dalmally 37 E3
Dalmellington 33 F4
Dalmeny 61 D4
Dalnavie 42 A2
Dalry 33 E2
Dalrymple 33 E4
Dalserf 61 F3
Dalston 29 F2
Dalton *Lancs.* **58 B1**
Dalton *S.Yorks.* 26 A4
Dalton *S.Yorks.* **57 E3**
Dalton-in-Furness 24 B1
Dalwhinnie 38 A1
Damerham 8 C3
Danbury 16 C4
Danby 31 E4
Danehill 10 B3
Darenth 53 G4
Daresbury 58 C3
Darfield 26 A4
Darlaston 54 B2
Darlington 31 D3
Darnall 57 D4
Darra 43 E3
Dartford 10 C1
Dartford 53 G4
Dartington 5 D2
Dartmeet 4 C2
Dartmouth 5 D3
Darton 26 A3
Darvel 33 F3
Darwen 25 D3
Datchet 52 A4
Daubhill 59 E1
Dava 42 B3
Davenham 20 A1
Davenham 59 D4
Daventry 15 D1
Daviot 42 A3
Dawlish 5 D2
Deal 11 F2
Dean *Hants.* **50 C1**
Dean Row 59 F3
Dearham 29 E3
Debenham 17 E1
Dechmont 34 A1
Deddington 15 D2
Dedham 17 D2
Deeping St. James 22 A3
Deeping St. Nicholas 22 A3
Deganwy 18 C1
Delabole 4 A1
Delamere 19 F2
Delamere 58 C5
Denaby 57 E3
Denaby Main 57 E3
Denbigh 19 D2
Denby 56 A1
Denby Dale 25 F3
Denham *Bucks.* 10 A1
Denham *Bucks.* **52 B3**
Denham Green 52 B3
Denholm 35 D3
Denholme 25 F2
Denmead 9 E3

Denmead 50 A3
Dennington 17 E1
Denny 34 A1
Denton 25 E4
Denver 22 C4
Denvilles 50 B4
Deptford *Gt.Lon.* **53 E4**
Derby 21 D2
Derby 56 A2
Dersingham 22 C3
Dervaig 36 C2
Desborough 21 E4
Devil's Bridge 12 C2
Devizes 8 C1
Dewsbury 25 F3
Dewsbury 57 E2
Dhoon 24 B2
Diabaig 40 C2
Dibden 9 D3
Dibden 50 B2
Dibden Purlieu 50 B2
Didcot 15 D4
Didling 50 C3
Didsbury 59 F2
Digmoor 58 B1
Dilhorne 56 C4
Dinas Powys 7 E2
Dinas Powys 51 D2
Dingwall 41 F2
Dinnington *S.Yorks.* **26 B4**
Dinnington *S.Yorks.* **57 E4**
Dinnington *T. & W.* **60 A1**
Dippen 32 C3
Dirleton 34 C1
Diss 17 E1
Distington 29 E3
Ditton *Ches.* **58 B3**
Ditton *Kent* 11 D2
Dobwalls 4 A2
Dochgarroch 41 F3
Docking 22 C2
Doddinghurst 53 G2
Doddington 35 E3
Dodford *H. & W.* **54 B4**
Dodington 14 A4
Dodworth 26 A4
Dogdyke 22 A2
Dolanog 13 E1
Dolbenmaen 18 B3
Dolfor 13 E2
Dolgarrog 18 C2
Dolgellau 12 C1
Dollar 38 B4
Dolphinton 34 B2
Doncaster 26 B4
Donington 22 A2
Donkey Town 52 A5
Donnington *Shrop.* 20 A3
Donnington *W.Suss.* **50 C4**
Dorchester 8 A4
Dordon 20 C4
Dordon 55 E1
Dore 57 D4
Dores 41 F3
Dorket Head 56 C1
Dorking 10 B2
Dormanstown 60 C4
Dorney 52 A4
Dornie 41 D3
Dornoch 42 A1
Dorridge 55 D4
Dosthill 55 E1
Dougalston 61 D1
Dougarie 32 C3
Douglas *I.o.M.* 24 B3
Douglas *S.Lan.* 34 A3
Douglastown 39 D2
Dounby 49 D3
Doune 38 B4
Dounreay 45 E1

Dover 11 F3
Doverdale 54 A5
Doveridge 20 C2
Dowally 38 C2
Downe 53 F5
Downham Market 22 C4
Downholland Cross 58 A1
Downton 8 C2
Dowsby 22 A3
Draethen 51 E1
Drakes Cross 54 C4
Draycott *Derbys.* **56 B2**
Drayton *Hants.* **50 A4**
Drayton *Norf.* 23 E3
Drayton *Oxon.* 15 D4
Drayton Bassett 55 D1
Drefach 6 B1
Dreghorn 33 E3
Drem 34 C1
Drighlington 57 E2
Drimnin 36 C2
Droitwich 14 B1
Droitwich 54 A5
Dronfield 21 D1
Drongan 33 F3
Dropmore 52 A3
Droxford 50 A3
Droylsden 25 E4
Druid 19 D3
Druidrishaig 32 C1
Drumbeg 44 A2
Drumchapel 61 D1
Drumclog 33 F3
Drumlithie 39 F1
Drummore 28 A2
Drumnadrochit 41 F3
Drybrook 14 A3
Drymen 33 F1
Duddingston 61 E4
Duddo 35 E2
Duddon 58 C5
Dudley *T. & W.* **60 A1**
Dudley *W.Mid.* 20 B4
Dudley *W.Mid.* **54 B2**
Dudley Hill 57 D1
Dudley Port 54 B2
Duffield 21 D2
Duffield 56 A1
Dufftown 42 C3
Duirinish 40 C3
Dullatur 61 F1
Dullingham 16 C2
Dulnain Bridge 42 B3
Dulverton 7 D4
Dulwich 53 E4
Dumbarton 33 E1
Dumfries 29 D1
Dunbar 35 D1
Dunbeath 45 E3
Dunblane 38 B4
Dunchurch 15 D1
Dundee 39 D3
Dundonald 33 E3
Dundreggan 41 E4
Dundrennan 29 D2
Dunecht 43 E4
Dunfermline 34 B1
Dunham-on-the-Hill 58 B4
Dunhampton 54 A5
Dunham Town 59 E3
Dunholme 21 F1
Dunkeld 38 C3
Dunkirk 11 E2
Dunlop 33 E2
Dunnet 45 E1
Dunning 38 C4
Dunoon 33 D1
Dunragit 28 A2
Duns 35 D2
Dunscore 29 D1

Dunstable 15 F3
Dunster 7 D3
Dunston *T. & W.* **60 A2**
Dunton Wayletts 53 H3
Dunure 33 E4
Dunvant 6 C1
Dunvegan 40 A3
Durham 31 D2
Durley *Hants.* **50 C1**
Durness 44 B1
Durrington 8 C1
Dursley 14 A3
Dutton 58 C4
Dyce 43 E4
Dyke 42 B2
Dykehead 39 D2
Dymchurch 11 E3
Dymock 14 A2
Dyserth 19 D1

E

Eaglescliffe 31 D3
Eaglescliffe 60 B5
Eaglesfield 29 E1
Eaglesham 33 F2
Eaglesham 61 D3
Ealing 52 C3
Earby 25 E2
Eardisley 13 E3
Earith 16 B1
Earlestown 58 C2
Earls Barton 15 F1
Earls Colne 17 D3
Earlsdon 55 F4
Earlston 35 D3
Earl Shilton 21 D4
Earl Stonham 17 E2
Earlswood *Warks.* **55 D4**
Earsairidh 46 A4
Earsdon 60 B1
Easdale 37 D4
Easebourne 9 F2
Easington *Dur.* 31 D2
Easington *E.Riding* 27 E3
Easington Colliery 31 D2
Easingwold 26 B1
East Ardsley 57 F2
East Ashling 50 C4
East Barnet 52 D2
East Bedfont 52 B4
East Bergholt 17 D2
East Boldon 60 B2
East Boldre 50 B2
Eastbourne *Dur.* 60 A5
Eastbourne *E.Suss.* 10 C4
East Bridgford 21 E2
Eastbury *Herts.* **52 C2**
East Calder 34 B1
Eastcote *Gt.Lon.* **52 C3**
Eastcote *W.Mid.* **55 D4**
East Dereham 23 D3
East End *N.W.Som.* **51 E4**
Easter Compton 51 F3
Easter Lednathie 39 D2
Easter Quarff 48 B4
Eastfield 27 D1
Eastgate 30 B2
East Goscote 21 E3
East Grinstead 10 B3
East Ham 53 F3
East Hanney 15 D4
East Harling 23 D4
East Harting 50 B3
East Haven 35 E3
East Horndon 53 H3
East Horsley 10 A2
East Huntspill 7 F3
East Keal 22 B1
East Kilbride 33 F2

East Kilbride 61 E3
East Lavant 50 C4
East Leake 21 D3
Eastleigh *Hants.* 9 D3
Eastleigh *Hants.* **50 B1**
East Linton 35 D1
East Looe 4 B3
East Malling 11 D2
East Marden 50 C3
East Markham 21 E1
East Midlands Airport 21 D2
East Molesey 52 C5
Eastoft 26 C3
Easton 8 A4
Easton-in-Gordano 7 F2
Easton-in-Gordano 51 F4
Easton on the Hill 21 F3
East Preston 10 A4
Eastriggs 29 F1
Eastry 11 F2
East Wemyss 39 D4
East Wickham 53 F4
East Wittering 9 F3
Eastwood *Notts.* 21 D2
Eastwood *Notts.* **56 B1**
Eathorpe 55 F5
Eaton (Congleton) *Ches.* **59 F5**
Eaton (Tarporley) *Ches.* **58 C5**
Eaton Socon 16 A1
Ebbw Vale 7 E1
Ecclaw 35 D1
Ecclefechan 29 E1
Eccles *Bord.* 35 D2
Eccles *Gt.Man.* **59 E2**
Ecclesfield 26 A4
Ecclesfield 57 D3
Eccleshall 20 B2
Eccleston *Ches.* **58 B5**
Eccleston *Lancs.* 25 D3
Eccleston *Mers.* **58 B2**
Echt 43 E4
Eckford 35 D3
Eckington *Derbys.* 21 D1
Eckington *H. & W.* 14 B2
Edderton 42 A1
Eddleston 34 B2
Eddlewood 61 F3
Edenbridge 10 C2
Edenfield 25 E3
Eden Park 53 E5
Edgbaston 54 C3
Edgware 52 D2
Edgworth 25 D3
Edial 54 C1
Edinbarnet 61 D1
Edinburgh 34 B1
Edinburgh 61 E4
Edinburgh (Turnhouse)
  Airport 34 B1
Edinburgh (Turnhouse)
  Airport 61 D4
Edlingham 35 F4
Edmonton 53 E2
Edmundbyers 30 C2
Edney Common 53 H1
Edstone 55 D5
Edwalton 56 C2
Edwinstowe 21 E1
Edzell 39 E2
Egglescliffe 31 D3
Egglescliffe 60 B5
Egham 10 A1
Egham 52 B4
Eglingham 35 F3
Eglwys Fach 12 C1
Eglwyswrw 12 A4
Egremont 29 E3
Egton 31 F4
Einacleit 47 D2
Elberton 51 F3
Elgin 42 C2

Elgol 40 B4
Elham 11 E2
Elie 39 E4
Eling 50 A1
Elland 25 F3
Elland 57 D2
Ellesmere 19 E3
Ellesmere Port 19 F1
Ellesmere Port 58 A4
Ellingham 35 F3
Ellington 35 F4
Ellon 43 F3
Elloughton 26 C3
Elm 22 B4
Elmbridge 54 B5
Elmdon *W.Mid.* **55 D3**
Elmdon Heath 55 D3
Elmley Lovett 54 A5
Elm Park 53 G3
Elmswell 17 D1
Elmton 21 D1
Elphin 44 B3
Elphinstone 61 F4
Elsdon 35 E4
Elsrickle 34 B2
Elstead 9 F2
Elsted 50 C3
Elstob 60 A4
Elstree 16 A4
Elstree 52 C2
Elswick 24 C2
Eltham 53 F4
Elton *Cambs.* 22 A4
Elton *Ches.* 19 F1
Elton *Ches.* **58 B4**
Elton *Stock.* **60 B5**
Elvanfoot 34 A3
Elvaston 56 B2
Elvington 26 B2
Ely *Cambs.* 16 B1
Ely *Cardiff* 7 E2
Ely *Cardiff* **51 D2**
Embleton 35 F3
Emsworth 9 F3
Emsworth 50 B4
Enderby 21 D4
Endon 20 B2
Endon 56 C3
Enfield 53 E2
Englefield Green 52 A4
Englesea-brook 56 A3
Enstone 15 D2
Enterkinfoot 34 A4
Enville 54 A3
Eoropaidh 47 F1
Epping 16 B4
Epping 53 F1
Epping Green *Essex* **53 F1**
Epping Green *Herts.* **52 D1**
Epping Upland 53 F1
Epsom 10 B2
Epsom 52 D5
Epworth 26 C4
Erdington 55 D2
Eriboll 44 B2
Eriswell 16 C1
Erith 53 G4
Errogie 41 F4
Errol 39 D3
Esher 10 A2
Esher 52 C5
Esh Winning 30 C2
Eskdalemuir 34 B4
Essendon 52 D1
Essington 54 B1
Eston 31 E3
Eston 60 C5
Eton 10 A1
Eton 52 A4
Eton Wick 52 A4

Etteridge 38 A1
Ettingshall 54 B2
Ettington 14 C2
Ettrick 34 B4
Ettrickbridge 34 C3
Euxton 25 D3
Evanton 41 F2
Evercreech 8 A2
Evesham 14 B2
Ewell 10 B2
Ewell 52 D5
Ewhurst 10 A3
Exbury 50 B2
Exebridge 7 D4
Exeter 5 D1
Exminster 5 D1
Exmouth 5 E2
Eye *Cambs.* 22 A4
Eye *Suff.* 17 E1
Eyemouth 35 E2
Eynsford 10 C2
Eynsford 53 G5
Eynsham 15 D3

F

Faifley 61 D1
Failand 51 F4
Failsworth 25 E4
Failsworth 59 F1
Fairford 14 C3
Fairholm 61 F3
Fairlie 33 E2
Fairlight 11 D4
Fair Oak *Hants.* 9 E3
Fair Oak *Hants.* **50 B1**
Fairseat 53 H5
Fakenham 23 D3
Falkirk 34 A1
Falkland 39 D4
Fallin 34 A1
Falmouth 3 F3
Falstone 30 A1
Fareham 9 E3
Fareham 50 C2
Faringdon 14 C4
Farington 25 D3
Farleigh *Surr.* **53 E5**
Farmborough 8 A1
Farnborough *Gt.Lon.* **53 F5**
Farnborough *Hants.* 9 F1
Farndon 21 E2
Farnham 9 F1
Farnham Common 52 A3
Farnham Royal 10 A1
Farnham Royal 52 A3
Farningham 53 G5
Farnsfield 21 E1
Farnworth *Ches.* **58 C3**
Farnworth *Gt.Man.* 25 D3
Farnworth *Gt.Man.* **59 E1**
Farr 42 A3
Farsley 57 E1
Fatfield 60 B3
Fauldhouse 34 A2
Faversham 11 E2
Fawdon 60 A2
Fawkham Green 53 G5
Fawley *Hants.* 9 D3
Fawley *Hants.* **50 B2**
Fazeley 20 C4
Fazeley 55 E1
Fearnhead 59 D2
Fearnmore 40 C2
Featherstone *Staffs.* **20 B3**
Featherstone *W.Yorks.* 26 A3
Felden 52 B1
Felindre 13 E2

Felixstowe 17 E2
Felling 31 D1
Felling 60 A2
Felsted 16 C3
Feltham 52 C4
Felton 35 F4
Feltwell 22 C4
Fence Houses 60 B3
Fen End 55 E4
Feniton 5 E1
Fenny Drayton 55 F2
Fenstanton 16 A1
Fenton *Staffs.* **56 B4**
Fenwick *E.Ayr.* 33 F2
Fenwick *Nhumb.* 35 F2
Feochaig 32 C4
Feolin Ferry 32 B2
Fern 39 E2
Ferndown 8 C3
Ferness 42 B3
Fernhill Heath 14 B1
Fernhurst 9 F2
Ferryden 39 E2
Ferryhill 31 D3
Feshiebridge 42 A4
Fettercairn 39 E1
Ffestiniog 18 C3
Ffostrasol 12 B3
Fiddington 8 A1
Fiddlers Hamlet 53 F1
Filey 27 D1
Fillongley 20 C4
Fillongley 55 E3
Filton 14 A4
Filton 51 F4
Fimber 26 C1
Finavon 39 E2
Finchampstead 9 F1
Finchdean 50 B3
Finchingfield 16 C3
Finchley 52 D2
Findern 20 C2
Findern 56 A2
Findhorn 42 B2
Findochty 43 D2
Findon 10 A4
Finedon 15 F1
Finningham 17 D1
Finningly 26 B4
Finnygaud 43 D2
Finsbury 53 E3
Finstall 54 B4
Finstown 49 E3
Fintry 33 F1
Fionnphort 36 B3
Firbeck 57 F4
Fir Vale 57 D4
Fishbourne *W.Suss.* **50 C4**
Fishburn 31 D3
Fishguard 12 B1
Fiunary 36 C2
Flackwell Heath 15 F4
Flamborough 27 D1
Flamstead End 53 E1
Flaunden 52 B1
Fleet 9 F1
Fleetwood 24 C2
Flemington 61 E3
Flempton 16 C1
Flimby 29 E3
Flimwell 11 D3
Flint 19 E1
Flitwick 15 F2
Flixton *Gt.Man.* **59 E2**
Flodden 35 E3
Flookburgh 24 C1
Fochabers 42 C2
Foleshill 55 F3
Folkestone 11 F3
Folkingham 21 F2
Folly Gate 4 C1

Ford *Arg. & B.* 35 E3
Ford *Mers.* **58 A1**
Ford *Nhumb.* 37 D4
Fordham 16 C1
Fordingbridge 8 C3
Fordoun 39 F1
Fordyce 43 D2
Forest Gate 53 F3
Forest Hall *T. & W.* **60 A2**
Forest Row 10 C3
Forestside 50 B3
Forfar 39 D2
Forgandenny 38 C3
Forgie 42 C2
Formby 24 C3
Forres 42 B2 ,
Forsbrook 20 B2
Forsbrook 56 C4
Forsinard 45 D2
Fort Augustus 41 E4'
Forth 34 A2
Fortingall 38 B2
Fortrose 42 A2
Fortuneswell 8 A4
Fort William 37 E1
Forty Green 52 A2
Forty Hill 53 E2
Foster Street 53 F1
Fotherby 27 E4
Foulden 35 E2
Foulridge 25 E2
Four Ashes *Staffs.* **54 B1**
Four Crosses *Staffs.* **54 B1**
Four Elms 10 C2
Fourlanes End 56 A3
Four Marks 9 E2
Four Oaks *E.Suss.* 11 D3
Four Oaks (Meriden) *W.Mid.*
55 E3
Four Oaks (Sutton Coldfield)
W.Mid. 55 D2
Fownhope 14 A2
Foxdale 24 A3
Foxton *Dur.* **60 A4**
Foxwist Green 59 D5
Foyers 41 F4
Framfield 10 C3
Framingham 17 E1
Frampton Cotterell 14 A4
Frampton on Severn 14 A3
Franche 54 A4
Frankley 20 B4
Frankley 54 B3
Fratton 50 A4
Freckleton 24 C3
Freemantle 50 B1
Fremington 6 B4
Freshwater 9 D4
Freshwater East 12 B2
Fressingfield 17 E1
Freswick 45 F1
Freuchie 39 D4
Fridaythorpe 26 C1
Friern Barnet 52 D2
Frimley 9 F1
Frinton-on-Sea 17 E3
Friockheim 39 E2
Frithelstock Stone 6 B4
Frizington 29 E3
Frodsham 19 F1
Frodsham 58 C4
Frogmore *Hants.* 9 F1
Frogmore *Herts.* **52 C1**
Frome 8 B2
Fryerning 53 H1
Fulbourn 16 B2
Fulford *Staffs.* **20 B2**
Fulford *York* 26 B2
Fulham 10 B1
Fulham 52 D4
Fulmer 52 A3

Fulwell *T. & W.* **60 B3**
Fulwood *S.Yorks.* 25 D2
Fulwood *S.Yorks.* **57 D4**
Funtington 50 C4
Funtley 50 C2
Funzie 48 C1
Furnace 37 E4
Fyfield *Essex* 16 B3
Fyfield *Essex* **53 G1**
Fyvie 43 E3

G

Gaer 13 E4
Gainford 30 C3
Gainsborough 26 C4
Gairloch 40 C1
Galashiels 34 C3
Galley Common 55 F2
Gallowstree Elm 54 A3
Galmisdale 36 C1
Galston 33 F3
Gamlingay 16 A2
Garden City 58 A5
Gardenstown 43 E2
Garderhouse 48 B3
Garelochhead 33 E1
Garforth 26 A2
Gargrave 25 E2
Garlieston 28 C2
Garsdale Head 30 B4
Garstang 24 C2
Garston 58 B3
Garswood 58 C2
Gartcosh 61 F2
Garth 13 D3
Garthmyl 13 E1
Gartocharn 33 E1
Garvald 35 D1
Garvamore 38 A1
Garvard 32 A1
Garve 41 F2
Gateacre 58 B3
Gateford 57 F4
Gatehouse of Fleet 28 C2
Gateshead 31 D1
Gateshead 60 A2
Gathurst 58 C1
Gatley 25 E4
Gatley 59 F3
Gatwick (London) Airport
10 B3
Gawsworth 59 F5
Gawthrop 30 A4
Gayton 21 C3
Gearraidh na h-Aibhne 47 E2
Geddington 21 F4
Gedney 22 B3
Gelligaer 7 E1
George Green 52 B3
Georgeham 6 B3
Gerrards Cross 10 A1
Gerrards Cross 52 A3
Gidea Park 53 G3
Giffnock 33 F2
Giffnock 61 D3
Gifford 34 C1
Gilberdyke 26 C3
Gildersome 57 E2
Gildingwells 57 F4
Gillamoor 31 E4
Gillingham *Dorset* 8 B2
Gillingham *Kent* 11 D2
Gilling West 30 C4
Gillow Heath 56 B3
Gilmerton 38 B3
Gilsland 30 A1
Gilston 34 C2
Gilwern 7 E1
Girlsta 48 B3
Girvan 33 E4

Gisburn 25 E2
Glamis 39 D2
Glan-y-llyn 51 D1
Glanaman 6 C1
Glanton 35 E3
Glasbury 13 E4
Glascote 55 E1
Glasgow 33 F2
Glasgow 61 D2
Glasgow Airport 33 F2
Glassford 33 F2
Glastonbury 7 F3
Glazebury 59 D2
Gleadless 57 D4
Gleadsmoss 59 F5
Gledhow 57 F1
Glemsford 16 C2
Glenbarr 32 B3
Glenbeg 36 C2
Glenboig 61 F2
Glenborrodale 36 C2
Glenbreck 34 B3
Glenbrittle 40 B4
Glencaple 29 E1
Glencarse 38 C3
Glencoe 37 E2
Gleneagles 38 B4
Glenegedale 32 A2
Glenelg 40 C4
Glenfarg 38 C4
Glenfield 21 D3
Glenfinnan 37 D1
Glengarnock 33 E2
Glenkindie 43 D4
Glenluce 28 A2
Glenmavis 61 F2
Glenrothes 39 D4
Glen Vine 24 A3
Glinton 22 A4
Glossop 25 F4
Gloucester 14 B3
Glusburn 25 E2
Glyn-Neath 7 D1
Glyn Ceiriog 19 E3
Glyncorrwg 7 D1
Gnosall 20 B3
Gobowen 19 E3
Godalming 10 A2
Godmanchester 16 A1
Godstone 10 B2
Goff's Oak 53 E1
Gogar 61 D4
Golborne 25 D4
Golborne 59 D2
Goldcliff 7 F2
Goldcliff 51 D3
Goldenhill 56 B3
Golden Pot 9 F2
Golders Green 52 D3
Golspie 45 D4
Gomersal 57 E2
Goodwick 12 A1
Goodyers End 55 F3
Goole 26 B3
Goonhavern 3 F2
Goostrey 59 E4
Gorcott Hill 54 C5
Gordon 35 D2
Gorebridge 34 C2
Goring 15 E4
Gornalwood 54 B2
Gorseinon 6 C1
Gorton Gt.Man. 59 F2
Gosberton 22 A3
Gosfield 16 C3
Gosforth Cumb. 29 E4
Gosforth T. & W. 30 C1
Gosforth T. & W. 60 A2
Gospel End 54 B2
Gosport 9 E3
Gotham 21 D2

Gotham 56 C2
Goudhurst 11 D3
Gourdon 39 F2
Govan 61 D2
Goxhill 27 D3
Grabhair 47 E2
Grain 11 D1
Grampound 3 F3
Grandtully 38 B2
Grange-over-Sands 24 C1
Grange Hill 53 F2
Grangemouth 34 A1
Grangetown Cardiff 51 D2
Grangetown R. & C. 60 C4
Grange Villa 60 A3
Grantham 21 F2
Grantown-on-Spey 42 B3
Grantshouse 35 D2
Grappenhall 59 D3
Grasmere 29 F4
Grassendale 58 A3
Grassington 25 E1
Gravelly Hill 55 D2
Gravesend 10 C1
Gravesend 53 H4
Grayrigg 30 A4
Grays 10 C1
Grays 53 H4
Grayshott 9 F2
Greasbrough 57 E3
Greasby 19 E1
Great Altcar 58 A1
Great Ayton 31 E3
Great Ayton 60 C5
Great Baddow 16 C3
Great Barr 54 C2
Great Barrow 58 B5
Great Barton 17 D1
Great Bircham 22 C3
Great Broughton 31 E4
Great Budworth 59 D4
Great Burdon 60 A5
Great Clifton 29 E3
Great Cornard 17 D2
Great Crosby 58 A1
Great Driffield 27 D2
Great Dunmow 16 C3
Great Eccleston 24 C2
Great Ellingham 23 D4
Great Glen 21 E4
Great Gonerby 21 F2
Great Gransden 16 A2
Greatham Hants. 9 F2
Greatham Hart. 60 B4
Great Hanwood 13 F1
Great Harwood 25 D2
Great Heath 55 F3
Great Horkesley 17 D3
Great Linford 15 F2
Great Malvern 14 A2
Great Marton 24 C2
Great Missenden 15 F3
Great Oxney Green 53 H1
Great Parndon 53 F1
Great Preston 57 E2
Great Salkeld 30 A2
Great Sampford 16 C2
Great Sankey 19 F1
Great Sankey 58 C3
Great Shelford 16 B2
Great Stainton 60 A4
Greatstone-on-Sea 11 E3
Great Sutton Ches. 58 A4
Great Torrington 6 B4
Great Wakering 11 E1
Great Warley 53 G2
Great Wyrley 20 B3
Great Wyrley 54 B1
Great Yarmouth 23 F4
Great Yeldham 16 C2

Greenford 52 C3
Greengairs 34 A1
Greengairs 61 F1
Greenham 9 E1
Greenhead 30 A1
Greenhill Gt.Lon. 52 C3
Greenhill S.Yorks. 57 D4
Greenhithe 53 G4
Greenigo 49 E3
Greenlaw 35 D2
Greenloaning 38 B4
Greenock 33 E1
Greensted 53 G1
Green Street 52 C2
**Green Street Green Gt.Lon.
    53 F5**
**Green Street Green Kent
    53 G4**
Greenway 12 A4
Greenwich 53 E4
Grendon Warks. 55 E2
Grendon Common 55 E2
Grenoside 57 D3
Gresford 19 E2
Gretna 29 F1
Greystoke 29 F3
Griais 47 F1
Griff 55 F3
Grimoldby 22 B1
Grimsby 27 D3
Grimston 22 C3
Gringley on the Hill 26 B4
Gritley 49 E3
Grizebeck 29 E4
Grove 15 D4
Grove Park 53 F4
Guide Post 30 C1
Guilden Sutton 58 B5
Guildford 10 A2
Guildtown 38 C3
Guisborough 31 E3
Guiseley 25 F2
Guist 23 D3
Gullane 34 C1
Gunness 26 C3
Gunnislake 4 B2
Gurnos 6 C1
Gutcher 48 C1
Gwaelod-y-garth 51 D1
Gwaun-Cae-Gurwen 6 C1
Gwithian 3 E3
Gwytherin 18 C2

H

Hackenthorpe 57 E4
Hackleton 15 E1
Hackling 11 F2
Hackness 31 F4
Hackney 53 E3
Haddenham 16 B1
Haddington 34 C1
Haddiscoe 23 F4
Hademore 55 D1
Hadleigh 17 D2
Hadley 20 A3
Hadley Wood 52 D2
Hadzor 54 B5
Hagley (Hereford) H. & W.
    14 A2
Hagley (Stourbridge) H. & W.
    20 B4
**Hagley (Stourbridge) H. & W.
    54 B3**
Haigh 59 D1
Hailsham 10 C4
Hainault 53 F2
Hale Gt.Man. 25 E4
Hale Gt.Man. 59 E3
Hale Bank 58 B3
Halebarns 59 E3

Hales 23 F4
Halesowen 20 B4
Halesowen 54 B3
Halesworth 17 F1
Halewood 19 F1
Halewood 58 B3
Halfpenny Green 54 A2
Halfway S.Yorks. 57 E4
Halifax 25 F3
Halkirk 45 E2
Halkyn 19 E1
Hall 33 E2
Halland 10 C4
Hallen 51 F4
Hallow 14 A1
Hallworthy 4 A1
Halmer End 56 A4
Halstead Essex 16 C3
Halstead Kent 53 F5
Halton Ches. 58 C3
Halton Gill 25 E1
Haltwhistle 30 A1
Halwell 5 D3
Ham Gt.Lon. 52 C4
Ham Shet. 48 A3
Hamble 50 A3
Hambledon Hants. 50 A3
Hambleton 24 C2
Hambrook W.Suss. 50 B4
Ham Green H. & W. 54 C5
Ham Green N.W.Som. 51 F4
Hamilton 33 F2
Hamilton 61 F3
**Hammersmith & Fulham
    52 C4**
Hammerwich 54 C1
Hammond Street 53 E1
Hamnavoe (Mainland) Shet.
    48 B4
Hamnavoe (Yell) Shet. 48 C2
Hampreston 8 C3
Hampstead 52 D3
Hampton Gt.Lon. 52 C5
Hampton in Arden 55 E3
Hampton Lovett 54 A5
Hampton on the Hill 55 E5
Hamstead W.Mid. 54 C2
Hamstreet 11 E3
Hanbury H. & W. 54 B5
Hanchurch 56 B4
Handbridge 58 B5
Handforth 59 F3
Handsacre 20 C3
Handsworth S.Yorks. 57 E4
Handsworth W.Mid. 54 C2
Hanford 56 B4
Hanham 14 A4
Hanley 56 B4
Hanley Castle 14 B2
Hanwell Gt.Lon. 52 C4
Hanworth Gt.Lon. 52 C4
Happisburgh 23 F3
Hapsford 58 B4
Harbledown 11 E2
Harborne 54 C3
Harbury 15 D1
Hardingstone 15 E1
Hardings Wood 56 B3
Hardley 50 B2
Hardway Hants. 50 A4
Hardwicke 14 A3
Harefield 10 A1
Harefield 52 B3
Harehills 57 F1
Hare Street 16 B3
Harewood 26 A2
Hargrave Ches. 58 B5
Haringey 53 E3
Harlech 18 B3
Harlesden 52 D3

Harleston 23 E4
Harlington 15 F2
Harlow 16 B3
Harmondsworth 52 B4
Harmston 21 F1
Harold Hill 53 G2
Haroldswick 48 C1
Harold Wood 53 G2
Harpenden 16 A3
Harpole 15 E1
Harpurhey 59 F1
Harrietfield 38 C3
Harrietsham 11 D2
Harriseahead 56 B3
Harrogate 26 A2
Harrow Gt.Lon. 52 C3
Harrow on the Hill 52 C3
Harrow Weald 52 C2
Harston 16 B2
Hartburn Stock. 60 B5
Hartfield 10 C3
Hartford Ches. 59 D4
Harthill N.Lan. 34 A2
Harthill S.Yorks. 57 E4
Hartland 6 A4
Hartlebury 14 B1
Hartlebury 54 A4
Hartlepool 31 E3
Hartley Kent 10 C2
Hartley Kent 53 H5
Hartley Wintney 9 F1
Harton T. & W. 60 B2
Hartpury 14 A2
Hartshill 21 D4
Hartshill 55 F2
Hartshorne 21 D3
Harvel 53 H5
Harvington H. & W. 14 B2
Harvington H. & W. 54 A4
Harwell 15 D4
Harwich 17 E3
Harworth 26 B4
Hasbury 54 B3
Haseley 55 E5
Haskayne 58 A1
Hasland 21 D1
Haslemere 9 F2
Haslington 56 A3
Hassall 56 A3
Hassall Green 56 A3
Hassendean 34 C3
Hastings 11 D4
Hastingwood 53 F1
Hastoe 52 A1
Haswell 31 D2
Hatch End 52 C2
Hatchmere 58 C4
Hatfield Herts. 16 A3
Hatfield Herts. 52 D1
Hatfield S.Yorks. 26 B3
Hatfield Broad Oak 16 B3
Hatfield Peverel 16 C3
Hatherleigh 4 C1
Hathern 21 D3
Hathersage 25 F4
Hatton Aber. 43 F3
Hatton Ches. 58 C3
Hatton Derbys. 20 C2
Hatton Gt.Lon. 52 B4
Hatton Warks. 55 E5
Haugh of Urr 29 D1
Haughton 20 B3
Haughton Le Skerne 60 A5
Havant 9 F3
Havant 50 B4
Haverfordwest 12 A2
Haverhill 16 C2
Havering 53 G3
Havering-atte-Bower 53 G2
Haverton Hill 60 B4

Hawarden 19 E2
Hawarden 58 A5
Hawarden Airport 58 A5
Hawes 30 B4
Hawick 34 C3
Hawkes End 55 F3
Hawkhurst 11 D3
Hawkinge 11 F3
Hawkshead 29 F4
Hawkwell 11 D1
Hawley *Hants.* 9 F1
Hawley *Kent* 53 G4
Haworth 25 F2
Haxby 26 B1
Haxey 26 C4
Hay-on-Wye 13 E3
Haydock 25 D4
Haydock 58 C2
Haydon Bridge 30 B1
Haydon Wick 14 C4
Hayes (Bromley) *Gt.Lon.*
　53 F5
Hayes (Hillingdon) *Gt.Lon.*
　52 B3
Hayfield 25 F4
Hayle 3 E3
Hay Mills 55 D3
Hayton 26 C2
Haywards Heath 10 B3
Hazel Grove 25 E4
Hazelwood *Derbys.* **56 A1**
Hazelwood *Gt.Lon.* **53 F5**
Hazlemere 15 F4
Hazlerigg 60 A1
Heacham 22 C2
Headless Cross 54 C5
Headley 9 F2
Heald Green 59 F3
Healeyfield 30 C2
Healing 27 D3
Heanor 21 D2
Heanor 56 B1
Heath 21 D1
Heathfield 10 C3
Heathrow (London) Airport
　10 A1
Heathrow (London) Airport
　52 B4
Heathton 54 A2
Heath Town 54 B2
Heatley 58 B3
Heaton *T. & W.* **60 A2**
Heaton Moor 59 F2
Hebburn 31 D1
Hebburn 60 B2
Hebden Bridge 25 E3
Hebden Green 59 D5
Heckington 22 A2
Heckmondwike 57 E2
Hedge End 9 E3
Hedge End 50 B1
Hedgerley 52 A3
Hedon 27 D3
Heeley 57 D4
Heglibister 48 B3
Heighington 21 F1
Helensburgh 33 E1
Helhoughton 23 D3
Hellifield 25 E2
Helmsdale 45 E3
Helmsley 31 E4
Helpringham 22 A2
Helsby 19 F1
Helsby 58 B4
Helston 3 E3
Hemel Hempstead 16 A3
Hemel Hempstead 52 B1
Hemingford Grey 16 A1
Hempnall 23 E4

Hempstead 16 C2
Hemsby 23 F3
Hemsworth 26 A3
Hemyock 7 E4
Henbury *Bristol* **51 F4**
Henbury *Ches.* **59 F4**
Hendon *Gt.Lon.* 10 B1
Hendon *Gt.Lon.* **52 D3**
Hendon *T. & W.* **60 B3**
Henfield 10 B4
Hengoed 7 E1
Henley-in-Arden 14 C1
Henley-in-Arden 55 D5
Henley-on-Thames 15 E4
Henlow 16 A2
Henstridge 8 B2
Hereford 13 F4
Heriot 34 C2
Hermiston 61 D4
Hermitage *W.Suss.* **50 B4**
Herongate 53 H2
Heronsgate 52 B2
Herrington 60 B3
Hersham *Surr.* **52 C5**
Herstmonceux 10 C4
Herston 49 E4
Hertford 16 B3
Heston 52 C4
Heswall 19 E1
Hethersett 23 E4
Hetton 25 E1
Hetton-le-Hole 31 D2
Hewell Grange 54 C5
Hewell Lane 54 C5
Hexham 30 B1
Hextable 10 C1
Hextable 53 G4
Heybridge (Ingatestone)
　Essex 53 H2
Heybridge (Maldon) *Essex*
　17 D3
Heysham 24 C1
Heyshott 50 C3
Heywood 25 E3
Hibaldstow 26 C4
Higham 11 D1
Higham Ferrers 15 F1
Higham on the Hill 55 F2
Highampton 4 B1
High Beach 53 F2
High Bentham 25 D1
High Blantyre 33 F2
High Blantyre 61 E3
High Bradfield 26 A4
Highbridge 7 E3
Highbury Vale 56 C1
Highclere 9 D1
Higher Blackley 59 F1
Higher Green 59 E2
Higher Walton *Ches.* 58 C3
Higher Walton *Lancs.* 25 D3
Higher Whitley 59 D3
High Etherley 30 C3
High Garrett 16 C3
High Green *S.Yorks.* **57 D3**
High Halden 11 D3
High Hawsker 31 F4
High Hesket 29 F2
Highlane *Ches.* **59 F5**
High Lane *Derbys.* **56 B1**
Highlane *Derbys.* **57 E4**
High Laver 53 G1
High Legh 25 D4
High Legh 59 E3
High Leven 60 B5
Highley 20 A4
High Lorton 29 E3
Highmoor Hill 51 E3
Highnam 14 A3
High Ongar 53 G1

Hightown *Ches.* **59 F5**
Highworth 14 C4
High Wycombe 15 F4
Hildenborough 10 C2
Hilgay 22 C4
Hill End 38 C4
Hill Head 50 C2
Hillingdon 52 B3
Hill of Fearn 42 A1
Hillpound 50 C1
Hillside *Angus* 39 E2
Hillside *Shet.* 48 B2
Hillswick 48 B2
Hill Top *Hants.* **50 B2**
Hilperton 8 B1
Hilsea 50 A4
Hilton *Derbys.* 20 C2
Hilton *Stock.* **60 B5**
Himley 54 A2
Hinckley 21 D4
Hinderwell 31 F3
Hindhead 9 F2
Hindley 25 D4
Hindley 59 D1
Hindley Green 59 D1
Hindon 8 B2
Hingham 23 D4
Hints *Staffs.* **55 D1**
Hipperholme 57 D2
Hirwaun 7 D1
Histon 16 B1
Hitchin 16 A3
Hither Green 53 E4
Hockley 11 D1
Hockley Heath 14 C1
Hockley Heath 55 D4
Hoddesdon 16 B3
Hoddesdon 53 E1
Hodnet 19 F3
Hoe Gate 50 A3
Hogsthorpe 22 B1
Holbeach 22 B3
Holbrook *Derbys.* **56 A1**
Holbrook *Suff.* 17 E2
Holden 25 E2
Holland-on-Sea 17 E3
Hollington 11 D4
Hollingworth 25 F4
Hollins 59 F1
Hollins Green 59 D2
Hollybush *E.Ayr.* 33 E4
Hollybush *H. & W.* 14 A2
Holme-on-Spalding-Moor
　26 C2
Holmes Chapel 20 A1
Holmes Chapel 59 E5
Holmesfield 20 C1
Holmfirth 25 F3
Holsworthy 4 B1
Holt *H. & W.* **54 A5**
Holt *Norf.* 23 D2
Holt *Wilts.* 8 B1
Holt *Wrex.* 19 F2
Holt End *H. & W.* **54 C5**
Holt Fleet 54 A5
Holt Heath *H. & W.* **54 A5**
Holtspur 52 A2
Holy Cross 54 B4
Holyhead 18 A1
Holytown 61 E3
Holywell 19 E1
Holywood 29 D1
Homersfield 17 E1
Honiley 55 E4
Honiton 5 E1
Honley 25 F3
Hoo 11 D1
Hook *E.Riding* 26 B3
Hook *Gt.Lon.* **52 C5**
Hook *Hants.* 9 F1

Hook Green (Meopham) *Kent*
　53 H5
Hook Green (Southfleet) *Kent*
　53 H4
Hook Norton 15 D2
Hoole 58 B5
Hooton 58 A4
Hooton Levitt 57 F3
Hooton Roberts 57 E3
Hope 19 E2
Hopeman 42 B2
Hopton *Norf.* 23 F4
Hopton *Suff.* 17 D1
Hopwas 55 D1
Hopwood 54 C4
Horam 10 C3
Horbling 22 A3
Horbury 26 A3
Horden 31 D2
Horeb 12 B3
Horfield 51 F4
Horley 10 B2
Hornby 25 D1
Horncastle 22 A1
Hornchurch 53 G3
Horndean *Hants.* 9 E3
Horndean *Hants.* **50 B3**
Horndon on the Hill 53 H3
Horn Hill 52 B2
Horning 23 E3
Hornsea 27 D2
Hornsey 53 E3
Horrabridge 4 C2
Horringer 16 C1
Horse Bridge 56 C3
Horsford 23 E3
Horsforth 57 E1
Horsham 10 B3
Horsley *Derbys.* **56 A1**
Horsley Woodhouse 56 A1
Horsmonden 11 D3
Horstead 23 E3
Horton *Berks.* **52 B4**
Horton *Staffs.* **56 C3**
Horton Heath 9 E3
Horton Heath 50 B1
Horton in Ribblesdale 25 E1
Horton Kirby 53 G5
Horwich 25 D3
Houbie 48 C1
Hough 56 A3
Hough Green 58 B3
Houghton le Spring 31 D2
Houghton Regis 15 F2
Hound 50 B2
Houndslow 35 D2
Hounsdown 50 A1
Hounslow 52 C4
Houston 33 E2
Houton 49 E3
Hove 10 B4
Hoveton 23 E3
Hovingham 26 B1
Howden 26 B3
Howwood 33 E2
Hoylake 19 E1
Hoyland 26 A4
Hucclecoat 21 D2
Hucknall 56 C1
Huddersfield 25 F3
Huggate 26 C2
Huish Episcopi 7 F4
Huisinis 47 D3
Hullavington 14 B4
Hullbridge 11 D1
Hulme Walfield 59 F5
Humberside Airport 27 D3
Humberston 27 E4
Humbie 34 C2
Hundleby 22 B1

Hundleton 12 A2
Hundred Acres 50 C1
Hungerford 9 D1
Hunmanby 27 D1
Hunningham 55 F5
Hunstanton 22 C2
Hunston *W.Suss.* 50 C4
Hunt's Cross 58 B3
Hunt End 54 C5
Hunter's Quay 33 E1
Huntingdon 16 A1
Huntly 43 D3
Hurley *Warks.* 55 E2
Hurlford 33 F3
Hursley 9 D2
Hurstbourne Tarrant 9 D1
Hurst Green 11 D3
Hurstpierpoint 10 B3
Hurworth-on-Tees 31 D3
Hurworth-on-Tees 60 A5
Husbands Bosworth 21 E4
Huttoft 22 B1
Hutton *Essex* **53 H2**
Hutton Cranswick 27 D2
Hutton Rudby 31 D4
Huyton 19 F1
Huyton 58 B2
Hyde 25 E4
Hyde Heath 52 A1
Hythe *Hants.* 9 D3
Hythe *Hants.* **50 B2**
Hythe *Kent* 11 E3
Hythe End 52 B4

I

Ibstock 21 D3
Ickenham 52 B3
Icklesham 11 D4
Icklingham 16 C1
Idrigil 40 B2
Ilchester 7 F4
Ilford 10 C1
Ilford 53 F3
Ilfracombe 6 B3
Ilkeston 21 D2
Ilkeston 56 B1
Ilkley 25 F2
Illey 54 B3
Ilminster 7 F4
Immingham 27 D3
Ince 58 B4
Ince-in-Makerfield 58 C1
Ince Blundell 58 A1
Inchbare 39 E2
Inchnadamph 44 B3
Inchture 39 D3
Ingatestone 16 C4
Ingatestone 53 H1
Ingleby Barwick 60 B5
Ingleton *Dur.* 30 C3
Ingleton *N.Yorks.* 25 D1
Inglewhite 25 D2
Ingoldmells 22 B1
Ingrave 53 H2
Ingst 51 F3
Inkberrow 14 B1
Innellan 33 D2
Innerleithen 34 C3
Insch 43 D3
Intake 57 D4
Inverallligan 40 C2
Inverallochy 43 F2
Inverarity 39 D3
Inverarnan 37 F4
Inverbervie 39 F1
Invercassley 44 C4
Invercharnan 37 E2
Inveresk 61 F4
Inverey 38 C1

Invergarry 41 E4
Invergordon 42 A2
Inverinan 37 E4
Inverkeilor 39 E2
Inverkeithing 34 B1
Inverkirkaig 44 A3
Inverlael 41 E1
Invermoriston 41 F4
Inverness 42 A3
Inverness (Dalcross) Airport 42 A2
Invernoaden 37 E4
Inverurie 43 E4
Ipplepen 5 D2
Ipstones 20 B2
Ipswich 17 E2
Irchester 15 F1
Irlam 25 D4
Irlam 59 E2
Ironbridge 20 A3
Irthlingborough 15 F1
Irvine 33 E3
Isbister (Mainland) Shet. 48 B1
Isbister (Whalsay) Shet. 48 C2
Isleham 16 C1
Isle of Man (Ronaldsway) Airport 24 A3
Isle of Whithorn 28 C2
Isleworth 52 C4
Islington 53 E3
Istead Rise 53 H5
Itchen 50 B1
Iver 10 A1
Iver 52 B3
Iver Heath 52 B3
Ivinghoe 15 F3
Ivybridge 4 C3
Iwade 11 D2
Ixworth 17 D1

J

Jackton 61 D3
Jarrow 31 D1
Jarrow 60 B2
Jaywick 17 E3
Jedburgh 35 D3
Jemimaville 42 A2
Jesmond 60 A2
Jodrell Bank 59 E4
John o' Groats 45 F1
Johnston 12 A2
Johnstone 33 E2
Johnstonebridge 34 B4
Joppa Edin. 61 F4
Jordans 52 A2

K

Kames 33 D1
Kearsley 25 D4
Kearsley 59 E1
Keckwick 58 C3
Kedington 16 C2
Kedleston 56 A1
Keelby 27 D3
Keele 20 A2
Keele 56 B4
Kegworth 21 D3
Keighley 25 F2
Keillmore 32 C1
Keiss 45 F1
Keith 43 D2
Kellas Angus 39 D3
Kellas Moray 42 C2
Kelsall 58 C5
Kelso 35 D3
Kelty 38 C4
Kelvedon 17 D3
Kelvedon Hatch 16 B4

Kelvedon Hatch 53 G2
Kemnay 43 E4
Kempsey 14 B2
Kempston 15 F2
Kendal 30 A4
Kenilworth 14 C1
Kenilworth 55 E4
Kenmore 38 B2
Kennacraig 32 C2
Kennethmont 43 D3
Kennington 15 D3
Kennoway 39 D4
Kensaleyre 40 B2
Kensington & Chelsea 52 D4
Kenswoth 15 F3
Kentallen 37 E2
Kenton Devon 5 D2
Kenton T. & W. 60 A2
Kenyon 59 D2
Keresley 55 F3
Kesgrave 17 E2
Kessingland 23 F4
Keston 53 F5
Keswick 29 F3
Kettering 21 F4
Kettlebrook 55 E1
Kettletoft 49 F2
Kettlewell 25 E1
Ketton 21 F3
Kew 52 C4
Kewstoke 7 F2
Key Green 59 F5
Keyingham 27 D3
Keymer 10 B4
Keynsham 8 A1
Keyworth 21 E2
Kibblesworth 60 A3
Kibworth Harcourt 21 E4
Kiddal Lane End 57 F1
Kiddemore Green 54 A1
Kidderminster 20 B4
Kidderminster 54 A4
Kidlington 15 D3
Kidsgrove 20 B2
Kidsgrove 56 B3
Kidwelly (Cydweli) 6 B1
Kielder 35 D4
Kilberry 32 C2
Kilbirnie 33 E2
Kilburn Derbys. 21 D2
Kilburn Derbys. 56 A1
Kilcadzow 34 A2
Kilchattan 34 A1
Kilchattan 36 B4
Kilchenzie 32 C3
Kilchiaran 32 A2
Kilchoan 36 C2
Kilchoman 32 A2
Kilchrenan 37 E3
Kilconquhar 39 E4
Kilcreggan 33 E1
Kildonan Lodge 45 D3
Kilfinan 33 D1
Kilgetty 6 A1
Kilham E.Riding 27 D1
Kilham Nmbh. 35 E3
Kilkhampton 6 A4
Killamarsh 26 A4
Killamarsh 57 E4
Killay 6 C1
Killean 32 C2
Killearn 33 F1
Killichonan 38 A2
Killiecrankie 38 B2
Killin 38 A3
Killinghall 26 A1
Killingworth 31 D1
Killingworth 60 A1
Killundine 36 C2
Kilmacolm 33 E1

Kilmalieu 37 D2
Kilmaluag 40 B2
Kilmarnock 33 F3
Kilmartin 37 D4
Kilmaurs 33 E3
Kilmelford 37 D4
Kilmington 5 F1
Kilmory Arg. & B. 32 C1
Kilmory (Rum) High. 40 A4
Kilnhurst 57 E3
Kilninian 36 B2
Kilninver 37 D3
Kiloran 36 B4
Kilrenny 39 E4
Kilsyth 33 F1
Kilwinning 33 E2
Kimberley Norf. 23 D4
Kimberley Notts. 21 D2
Kimberley Notts. 56 C1
Kimbolton 16 A1
Kimpton 16 A3
Kinbrace 45 D3
Kincardine 34 A1
Kincardine O'Neil 43 D4
Kincraig 42 A4
Kineton Green 55 D3
King's Heath 54 C3
King's Hill 54 B2
King's Lynn 22 C3
King's Norton W.Mid. 54 C4
King's Sutton 15 D2
King's Worthy 9 E2
Kingarth 33 D2
Kinghorn 34 B1
Kinglassie 39 D4
Kingsbarns 39 E4
Kingsbridge 4 C3
Kingsbury Gt.Lon. 52 C3
Kingsbury Warks. 20 C4
Kingsbury Warks. 55 E1
Kingsbury Episcopi 7 F4
Kingsclere 9 E1
Kingsdown 11 F2
Kingshouse 38 A3
Kingskerswell 5 D2
Kings Langley 15 F3
Kings Langley 52 B1
Kingsley Ches. 19 F1
Kingsley Ches. 58 C4
Kingsley Staffs. 20 B2
Kingsnorth 11 E3
Kingstanding 54 C2
Kingsteignton 5 D2
Kingsthorne 13 F4
Kingston 42 C2
Kingston Bagpuize 15 D3
Kingstone 13 F4
Kingston Seymour 7 F2
Kingston upon Hull 27 D3
Kingston upon Thames 52 C4
Kingswear 5 D3
Kingswinford 54 A3
Kingswood S.Glos. 14 A4
Kingswood Surr. 10 B2
Kingswood Warks. 55 D4
Kington 13 E3
Kingussie 42 A4
Kinkell 61 E1
Kinloch 40 B4
Kinlochard 38 A4
Kinlochbervie 44 B2
Kinlocheil 37 E1
Kinlochewe 41 D2
Kinloch Hourn 41 D4
Kinlochleven 37 F2
Kinloch Rannoch 38 A2
Kinloss 42 B2
Kinmel Bay 19 D1
Kinross 38 C4
Kintbury 9 D1

Kintore 43 E4
Kintour 32 B2
Kintra 32 A2
Kinver 20 B4
Kinver 54 A3
Kippax 26 A3
Kippen 38 A4
Kirby Corner 55 E4
Kirby Muxloe 21 D3
Kirkbean 29 D2
Kirkbride 29 E2
Kirkburton 25 F3
Kirkby Mers. 24 C4
Kirkby Mers. 58 B2
Kirkby in Ashfield 21 D1
Kirkby Lonsdale 25 D1
Kirkby Malzeard 25 F1
Kirkbymoorside 31 E4
Kirkby Stephen 30 B4
Kirkcaldy 34 B1
Kirkcolm 28 A1
Kirkconnel 34 A4
Kirkcowan 28 B2
Kirkcudbright 28 C2
Kirk Hallam 56 B1
Kirkham 24 C2
Kirkhamgate 57 E2
Kirkinner 28 B2
Kirkintilloch 33 F1
Kirkintilloch 61 E1
Kirkleatham 60 C4
Kirklevington 60 B5
Kirkliston 34 B1
Kirkliston 61 D4
Kirk Michael 24 A2
Kirkmichael P. & K. 38 C2
Kirkmichael S.Ayr. 33 E4
Kirkmuirhill 34 A2
Kirknewton Nmbh. 35 E3
Kirknewton W.Loth. 34 B2
Kirkoswald Cumb. 30 A2
Kirkoswald S.Ayr. 33 E4
Kirkpatrick-Fleming 29 F1
Kirkpatrick Durham 29 D1
Kirk Sandall 26 B3
Kirkstall 57 E1
Kirkton 37 D4
Kirkton of Culsalmond 43 D3
Kirkton of Durris 39 F1
Kirkton of Glenisla 39 D2
Kirkton of Kingoldrum 39 D2
Kirkton of Menmuir 39 E2
Kirkton of Skene 43 E4
Kirktown of Auchterless 43 E3
Kirktown of Deskford 43 D2
Kirkwall 49 E3
Kirk Yetholm 35 E3
Kirriemuir 39 D2
Kirtlington 15 D3
Kirton Lincs. 22 A2
Kirton Suff. 17 E2
Kirton in Lindsey 26 C4
Kiveton Park 57 E4
Knaresborough 26 A2
Knayton 31 D4
Knebworth 16 A3
Knighton 13 E2
Knock 36 C3
Knockandhu 42 C4
Knockban 41 E2
Knolls Green 59 F4
Knottingley 26 A3
Knotty Ash 58 B2
Knotty Green 52 A2
Knowle W.Mid. 20 C4
Knowle W.Mid. 55 D4
Knowsley 58 B2
Knucklas 13 E2
Knutsford 20 A1
Knutsford 59 E4

Knypersley 56 B3
Kyleakin 40 C3
Kyle of Lochalsh 40 C3
Kylerhea 40 C4
Kylestrome 44 B2

L

Laceby 27 D4
Lach Dennis 59 E4
Lacock 8 B1
Ladybank 39 D4
Ladykirk 35 E2
Ladysford 43 E2
Lagg 33 D3
Laggan (Invergarry) High. 37 F1
Laggan (Newtonmore) High. 38 A1
Lagganulva 36 C3
Laide 41 D1
Laindon 53 H3
Lairg 44 C4
Lakenheath 16 C1
Laleham 52 B5
Laleston 7 D2
Lamberhurst 11 D3
Lambeth 52 D4
Lambourn 9 D1
Lambourne End 53 F2
Lamesley 60 A3
Lamlash 33 D3
Lampeter 12 C3
Lamport 15 E1
Lanark 34 A2
Lancaster 24 C1
Lanchester 30 C2
Landore 6 C1
Landywood 54 B1
Lane End Bucks. 15 E4
Lane End Kent 53 G4
Lane Green 54 A1
Lane Head Gt.Man. 59 D2
Langdon Hills 53 H3
Langford 16 A2
Langham 21 F3
Langholm 29 F1
Langley Berks. 52 B4
Langley Derbys. 56 B1
Langley Hants. 50 B2
Langley Warks. 55 D5
Langley Mill 56 B1
Langold 26 B4
Langold 57 E4
Langport 7 F4
Langstone 50 B4
Langtoft 26 C1
Langwathby 30 A3
Lanivet 4 A2
Lapworth 14 C1
Lapworth 55 D4
Larbert 34 A1
Largoward 39 E4
Largs 33 E2
Larkhall 34 A2
Larkhall 61 F3
Larkhill 8 C1
Larling 23 D4
Latchford 59 D3
Latchingdon 17 D4
Lately Common 59 D2
Latheron 45 E2
Latheronwheel 45 E3
Latimer 52 B2
Lauder 34 C2
Laugharne 6 B1
Laughton-en-le-Morthen 57 F4
Launceston 4 B1
Laurencekirk 39 E2
Laurieston 28 C1

Lavenham 17 D2
Law 34 A2
Lawers 38 A3
Lawford 17 D3
Laxey 24 B2
Laxford Bridge 44 B2
Laxo 48 B2
Layer de la Haye 17 D3
Lazenby 60 C4
Lazonby 30 A2
Leadburn 34 B2
Leadenham 21 F2
Leadgate 30 C2
Leadhills 34 A3
Lea Marston 55 E2
Leasingham 21 F2
Leatherhead 10 A2
Leavening 26 C1
Leaves Green 53 F5
Lechlade 14 C3
Leckhampton 14 B3
Leckmelm 41 E1
Leckwith 51 D2
Ledaig 37 D3
Ledbury 14 A2
Ledmore 44 B3
Ledsham *Ches.* **58 A4**
Lee *Hants.* **50 A1**
Lee *Lancs.* 25 D2
Lee-on-the-Solent 9 E3
Lee-on-the-Solent 50 C2
Leeds *W.Yorks.* **57 E1**
Leeds & Bradford Airport 25 F2
Leedstown 3 E3
Leek 20 B1
Leek 56 C3
Leek Wootton 55 E5
Leeming 31 D4
Lee Moor 4 C2
Leicester 21 E3
Leigh *Gt.Man.* 25 D4
Leigh *Gt.Man.* **59 D1**
Leighton Buzzard 15 F2
Leigh Woods 51 F4
Leiston 17 F1
Leith 34 B1
Leith 61 E4
Lenham 11 D2
Lennoxtown 33 F1
Lenzie 61 E1
Leominster 13 F3
Lerwick 48 B3
Lesbury 35 F4
Leslie 39 D4
Lesmahagow 34 A3
Leswalt 28 A1
Letchmore Heath 52 C2
Letchworth 16 A2
Letheringsett 23 D2
Letterston 12 B1
Letwell 57 F4
Leuchars 39 D3
Leumrabhagh 47 E3
Leven *E.Riding* 27 D2
Leven *Fife* 39 D4
Levenhall 61 F4
Levenshulme 59 F2
Levenwick 48 B4
Leverstock Green 52 B1
Lewes 10 B4
Leyburn 30 C4
Leycett 56 A4
Leyland 25 D3
Leysdown-on-Sea 11 E1
Leyton 53 E3
Lhanbryde 42 C2
Libberton 34 A2
Lichfield 20 C3

Lichfield 55 D1
Lickey 54 B4
Lickey End 54 B4
Lightwater 9 F1
Lightwater 52 A5
Lightwood 56 C4
Lilleshall 20 A3
Lilliesleaf 34 C3
Limekilnburn 61 F3
Limekilns 34 B1
Lincoln 21 F1
Lincomb 54 A5
Lindfield 10 B3
Lindores 39 D4
Linford *Essex* 11 D1
Linford *Essex* **53 H4**
Lingfield 10 B2
Linlithgow 34 A1
Linsidemore 41 F1
Linton 16 B2
Liphook 9 F2
Liskeard 4 B2
Liss 9 F2
Lisvane 51 D1
Liswerry 7 F2
Liswerry 51 D3
Litherland 24 C4
Litherland 58 A2
Little Aston 54 C2
Little Berkhamsted 52 D1
Littleborough 25 E3
Littlebourne 11 F2
Little Budworth 58 C5
Little Burstead 53 H2
Little Chalfont 52 A2
Little Clacton 17 E3
Little Common 11 D4
Little Crosby 58 A1
Littledean 14 A3
Little Downham 16 B1
Little Eaton 21 D1
Little Eaton 56 A1
Little End 53 G1
Littlehampton 10 A4
Little Hay 55 D1
Little Heath 55 F3
Little Hulton 59 E1
Little Laver 53 G1
Little Leigh 59 D4
Little Lever 59 E1
Littlemill *E.Ayr.* 33 F4
Littlemill *High.* 42 B2
Little Missenden 15 F3
Little Missenden 52 A2
Littlemore 15 D3
Little Oakley 17 E3
Littleover 56 A2
Little Parndon 53 F1
Little Paxton 16 A1
Little Plumstead 23 E3
Littleport 22 B4
Little Stainton 60 A4
Little Stanney 58 B4
Littlestone-on-Sea 11 E3
Little Sutton 58 A4
Little Thurrock 53 H4
Littleton *Ches.* **58 B5**
Littleton *Surr.* **52 B5**
Littleton-Severn 51 F3
Little Warley 53 H2
Little Wyrley 54 C1
Liverpool 19 E1
Liverpool 58 A2
Liverpool Airport 58 B3
Liversedge 25 F3
Liversedge 57 D2
Livingston 34 B1
Lizard 3 E4
Llanaelhaearn 18 B2
Llanarth 12 B3
Llanarthney 12 B4

Llanbadarn Fawr 12 C2
Llanbadrig 18 A1
Llanbedr 18 B3
Llanbedrog 18 A3
Llanberis 18 B2
Llanbethian 7 D2
Llandaff 51 D2
Llandaff North 51 D2
Llanddarog 12 B4
Llanddeiniolen 18 B2
Llandderfel 19 D3
Llanddowror 6 A1
Llandeilo 12 C4
Llandevenny 51 E3
Llandinam 13 D2
Llandissilio 12 A4
Llandough (Penarth) 51 D2
Llandovery 12 C4
Llandrillo 19 D3
Llandrindod Wells 13 E3
Llandudno 18 C1
Llandwrog 18 B2
Llandybie 12 C4
Llandysul 12 B4
Llanedeyrn 51 E1
Llanegwad 12 B4
Llanelli 6 B1
Llanelltyd 18 C3
Llanelly 13 E4
Llanerchymedd 18 B1
Llanfaelog 18 A1
Llanfair Caereinion 13 E1
Llanfairfechan 18 C1
Llanfairpwllgwyngyll 18 B1
Llanfair Talhaiarn 19 D1
Llanfihangel ar-arth 12 B4
Llanfihangel Rogiet 51 E3
Llanfyllin 19 D3
Llanfynydd 19 E2
Llangadfan 13 D1
Llangadog 12 C4
Llangefni 18 B1
Llangeler 12 B4
Llangelynin 12 C1
Llangendeirne 6 B1
Llangernyw 18 C2
Llangoed 18 B1
Llangollen 19 E3
Llangranog 12 B4
Llangunnor 12 B4
Llangurig 13 D2
Llangwm 12 B2
Llangynidr 13 E4
Llanharan 7 D2
Llanhilleth 7 E1
Llanidloes 13 D2
Llanilar 12 C2
Llanishen *Cardiff* 7 E2
Llanishen *Cardiff* **51 D1**
Llanllwchaiarn 13 E2
Llanllyfni 18 B2
Llanmartin 51 D3
Llannon 6 B1
Llanon 12 B3
Llanrhaeadr-ym-Mochnant 19 D3
Llanrhidian 6 B1
Llanrhystud 12 B2
Llanrug 18 B2
Llanrumney 7 E2
Llanrumney 51 E1
Llanrwst 18 C2
Llansamlet 6 C1
Llansannan 19 D2
Llansantffraid Glan Conwy 18 C1
Llansawel 12 C4
Llanstephan 6 B1
Llanthony 13 E4
Llantilio Pertholey 13 F4

Llantrisant *Mon.* 7 F1
Llantrisant *R.C.T.* 7 D2
Llantwit Major 7 D2
Llanuwchllyn 18 C3
Llanwddyn 19 D3
Llanwern 51 D3
Llanwnda 18 B2
Llanwnog 13 D1
Llanwrda 12 C4
Llanwrtyd Wells 13 D3
Llanybydder 12 B3
Llanynghenedl 18 A1
Llanystumdwy 18 B3
Lledrod 12 C2
Loanhead 34 B2
Loans 33 E3
Lochailort 37 D1
Lochaline 36 C3
Lochans 28 A2
Locharbriggs 29 E1
Lochawe 37 E3
Loch Baghasdail
(Lochboisdale) 46 B3
Lochcarron 41 D3
Lochdon 37 D3
Lochearnhead 38 A3
Lochend 41 F3
Lochgelly 38 C4
Lochgilphead 32 C1
Lochgoilhead 37 F4
Lochinver 44 B3
Lochmaben 29 E1
Loch na Madadh
(Lochmaddy) 46 B1
Lochranza 33 D2
Loch Sgioport 46 B3
Lochwinnoch 33 E2
Lockerbie 29 E1
Locking 7 F3
Locksbottom 53 F5
Locks Heath 9 F3
Locks Heath 50 C2
Lockton 31 F4
Loddon 23 E4
Lofthouse *W.Yorks.* 26 A3
Lofthouse *W.Yorks.* **57 F2**
Loftus 31 E3
Logan 33 F3
Loggerheads 20 A2
London 10 B1
London City Airport 53 F3
London Colney 16 A4
London Colney 52 C1
Long Ashton 7 F2
Long Ashton 51 F4
Long Bennington 21 F2
Longbenton 31 D1
Longbridge 60 A2
Longbridge *Warks.* **55 E5**
Longbridge *W.Mid.* **54 C4**
Longbridge Deverill 8 B2
Long Buckby 15 E1
Long Common 51 C1
Long Compton 14 C2
Long Crendon 15 E3
Longcross *Surr.* **52 A5**
Long Ditton 52 C5
Longdon 20 C3
Long Eaton 21 D2
Long Eaton 56 B2
Longfield 53 H5
Longfield Hill 53 H5
Longford *Gt.Lon.* **52 B4**
Longford *W.Mid.* **55 F3**
Longforgan 39 D3
Longframlington 35 F4
Long Hanborough 15 D3
Longhope *Glos.* 14 A3
Longhope *Ork.* 49 D4
Longhorsley 35 F4
Longhoughton 35 F3

Long Itchington 15 D1
Long Lawford 21 D4
Longmanhill 43 E2
Long Melford 17 D2
Longmorn 42 C2
Longnewton *Stock.* **60 A5**
Longniddry 34 C1
Long Preston 25 E1
Longridge 25 D2
Longsdon 56 B3
Longside 43 F3
Long Stratton 23 E4
Long Sutton *Lincs.* 22 B3
Long Sutton *Som.* 7 F4
Longton *Lancs.* 24 C3
Longton *Staffs.* **56 C4**
Longtown 29 F1
Loose 11 D2
Lopcombe Corner 9 D2
Loscoe 21 D1
Loscoe 56 B1
Lossiemouth 42 C2
Lostock Gralam 59 D4
Lostock Green 59 D4
Lostock Junction 59 D1
Lostwithiel 4 A2
Loth 49 F2
Lothmore 45 E3
Loughborough 21 D3
Loughor 6 C1
Loughton *Essex* 16 B4
Loughton *Essex* **53 F2**
Louth 22 A1
Lovedean 50 A3
Loversall 57 F3
Loves Green 53 H1
Lowdham 21 E2
Low Dinsdale 60 A5
Lower Beeding 10 B3
Lower Cam 14 A3
Lower Failand 51 F4
Lower Green *Staffs.* **54 B1**
Lower Killeyan 32 A3
Lower Machen 51 E1
Lower Nazeing 53 E1
Lower Penarth 51 D2
Lower Penn 54 A2
Lower Peover 59 E4
Lower Swanwick 50 B2
Lower Upham 50 C1
Lower Walton 59 D3
Lower Whitley 59 D4
Lower Withington 59 F5
Lowestoft 23 F4
Loweswater 29 E3
Low Habberley 54 A4
Lowick 35 E3
Lowsonford 55 D5
Low Street 23 E3
Lowton 59 D2
Lowton Common 59 D2
Low Waters 61 F3
Ludag 46 A3
Luddesdown 53 H5
Ludgershall 9 D1
Ludgvan 3 D3
Ludlow 13 F2
Luggiebank 61 F1
Luib 40 B3
Lumphanan 43 D4
Luncarty 38 C3
Lundin Links 39 D4
Lunt 58 A1
Luss 33 E1
Lusta 40 A2
Luton 16 A3
Luton Airport 16 A3
Lutterworth 21 D4
Luxulyan 4 A3
Lybster 45 F3
Lydd 11 E3

Lydd Airport 11 E3
Lydford 4 C1
Lydiate 24 C4
Lydiate 58 A1
Lydney 14 A3
Lye **54 B3**
Lye Green 52 A1
Lymekilns 61 E3
Lyme Regis 5 F1
Lyminge 11 E3
Lymington 9 D3
Lymm 25 D4
Lymm 59 D3
Lympne 11 E3
Lympstone 5 D2
Lyndhurst 9 D3
Lyndhurst 50 A2
Lyne **Surr. 52 B5**
Lyneham 14 B4
Lynemore 42 B3
Lynemouth 35 F4
Lyne of Skene 43 E4
Lyness 49 D4
Lynmouth 6 C3
Lynton 6 C3
Lytchett Matravers 8 B3
Lytchett Minster 8 C3
Lytham St. Anne's 24 C3

M

Mablethorpe 22 B1
Macclesfield 20 B1
Macduff 43 E2
Machan 61 F3
Macharioch 32 C4
Machen 7 E1
Machen 51 E1
Machrihanish 32 B3
Machynlleth 12 C1
Mackworth 56 A2
Macmerry 34 C1
Madeley *Staffs.* 20 A2
Madeley *Staffs.* 56 A4
Madeley Heath 56 A4
Madley 13 F4
Madron 3 D3
Maenclochog 12 A4
Maentwrog 18 C3
Maerdy 7 D1
Maes-glas 51 E1
Maesteg 7 D1
Magdalen Laver 53 G1
Maghull 24 C4
Maghull 58 A1
Magor 51 E3
Maiden Bradley 8 B2
Maidenhead 15 F4
Maiden Newton 8 A3
Maidens 33 E4
Maidstone 11 D2
Malden 52 D5
Malden Rushett 52 C5
Maldon 17 D4
Malletsheugh 61 D3
Mallwyd 13 D1
Malmesbury 14 B4
Malpas 7 E1
Malpas 19 F2
Maltby *S.Yorks.* 26 B4
Maltby *S.Yorks.* 57 F3
Maltby *Stock.* 60 B5
Maltby le Marsh 22 B1
Malton 26 C1
Malvern Link 14 A2
Manby 22 B1
Mancetter 20 C4
Mancetter 55 F2
Manchester 25 E4
Manchester 59 F2
Manchester Airport 25 E4

Manchester Airport 59 F3
Mancot Royal 58 A5
Manea 22 B4
Mangotsfield 14 A4
Manley 58 C4
Manningtree 17 E3
Manorbier 6 A1
Mansfield 21 D1
Mansfield Woodhouse 21 D1
Manston 8 B3
Maple Cross 52 B2
Mapperley 56 B1
**Mappleborough Green
54 C5**
Marazion 3 E3
March 22 B4
Marchwiel 19 E2
Marchwood 50 A1
Marden *Kent* 11 D2
Marden *T. & W.* 60 B1
Mareham le Fen 22 A2
Maresfield 10 C3
Margam 6 C2
Margaretting 53 H1
Margate 11 F1
Marham 22 C3
Mark 7 F3
Market Bosworth 21 D3
Market Deeping 22 A3
Market Drayton 20 A2
Market Harborough 21 E4
Market Lavington 8 C1
Market Rasen 27 D4
Market Weighton 26 C2
Markfield 21 D3
Markinch 39 D4
Marks Gate 53 F3
Marks Tey 17 D3
Markyate 15 F3
Marlborough 8 C1
Marldon 5 D2
Marley Hill 60 A3
Marlow 15 F4
Marlpool 56 B1
Marnhull 8 B2
Marple 25 E4
Marsden *T. & W.* 60 C2
Marsden *W.Yorks.* 25 F3
Marshfield *Newport* 51 E1
Marshfield *S.Glos.* 14 A4
Marske-by-the-Sea 31 E3
Marston *Ches.* 59 D4
Marston *Oxon.* 15 D3
Marston *Warks.* 55 E3
Marston Green 55 D3
Marston Magna 8 A2
Marston Moretaine 15 F2
Marthall 59 F4
Martham 23 F3
Martinscroft 59 D3
Martlesham 17 E2
Martley 14 A1
Martock 7 F4
Marton *Ches.* 59 F5
Marton *Middbro.* 60 C5
Marybank 41 F2
Maryhill *Glas.* 61 D2
Marykirk 39 E2
Marylebone *Gt.Lon.* 52 D3
Marylebone *Gt.Man.* 58 C1
Marypark 42 C3
Maryport 29 E2
Marywell 39 E1
Matlock 20 C1
Matlock Bath 20 C1
Mauchline 33 F3
Maud 43 E3
Maughold 24 B2
Maw Green 54 C2
Maxstoke 55 E3
Maybole 33 E4

Mayfield 20 C2
Mealsgate 29 E2
Meare 7 F3
Mearns 61 D3
Measham 21 D3
Medstead 9 E2
Meer End 55 E4
Meidrim 12 A4
Meigle 39 D3
Meikle Earnock 61 F3
Meikle Kilmory 33 D2
Meikleour 38 C3
Meir 56 C4
Melbourn 16 B2
Melbourne 21 D3
Melby 48 A3
Melksham 8 B1
Melling *Mers.* 58 A1
Melling Mount 58 B1
Melmerby 30 A2
Melrose 34 C3
Melsonby 30 C4
Meltham 25 F3
Melton 17 E2
Melton Mowbray 21 E3
Melvaig 40 C1
Melvich 45 D1
Memsie 43 F2
Menai Bridge 18 B1
Menston 25 F2
Menstrie 38 B4
Meon 50 C2
Meonstoke 50 A3
Meopham 53 H5
Meopham Green 53 H5
Mere *Ches.* 59 E3
Mere *Wilts.* 8 B2
Mere Green 55 D2
Meriden 20 C4
Meriden 55 E3
Merry Hill 52 C2
Merston 50 C4
Merton *Gt.Lon.* 52 D5
Merthyr Tydfil 7 D1
Merton *Gt.Lon.* 52 D5
Messingham 26 C3
Metfield 17 E1
Metheringham 21 F1
Methley 57 F2
Methlick 43 E3
Methven 38 C3
Methwold 22 C4
Mevagissey 4 A3
Mexborough 26 A4
Mexborough 57 E3
Mey 45 F1
Miabhig 47 D2
Michaelston-le-Pit 51 D2
Michaelston-y-Fedw 51 E1
Mickleover 56 A2
Mickleton *Dur.* 30 B3
Mickleton *Glos.* 14 C2
Mickletown 57 F2
Mickle Trafford 58 B5
Mid Ardlaw 43 F2
Midbea 49 E2
Middle Barton 15 D2
Middleham 30 C4
Middlemarsh 8 A3
Middle Rasen 27 D4
Middlesbrough 31 D3
Middlesbrough 60 B4
Middlesmoor 25 F1
Middleton *Gt.Man.* 25 E4
Middleton *Gt.Man.* 59 F1
Middleton *Norf.* 22 C3
Middleton *Warks.* 55 D2
Middleton *W.Yorks.* 57 E2
Middleton-in-Teesdale 30 B3
Middleton-on-Sea 10 A4
Middleton-on-the-Wolds
26 C2

Middleton Cheney 15 D2
Middleton One Row 60 A5
Middleton St. George 60 A5
Middleton Stoney 15 D3
Middlewich 20 A1
Middlewich 59 E5
Midhurst 9 F2
Mid Lavant 50 C4
Midlem 34 C3
Midsomer Norton 8 A1
Mid Yell 48 C1
Milborne Port 8 A2
Milborne St. Andrew 8 B3
Mildenhall 16 C1
Mile End 17 D3
Milfield 35 E3
Milford *Derbys.* 56 A1
Milford *Surr.* 9 F2
Milford Haven 12 A2
Milford on Sea 9 D4
Millbrook *Cornw.* 4 B3
Millbrook *Hants.* 50 A1
Mill Green *Essex* 53 H1
Mill Hill 52 D2
Millhouse 33 D1
Millport 33 D2
Milltown 43 D4
Milltown of Rothiemay 43 D3
Milnathort 38 C4
Milngavie 33 F1
Milngavie 61 D1
Milnrow 25 E3
Milovaig 40 A2
Milton *High.* 41 F3
Milton *Newport* 51 D3
Milton *P. & K.* 38 B3
Milton *Staffs.* 56 C3
Milton Keynes 15 F2
Milton of Campsie 33 F1
Milton of Campsie 61 E1
Milverton 7 E4
Minard 37 E4
Minchinhampton 14 B3
Minehead 7 D3
Minera 19 E2
Minnigaff 28 B1
Minster (Sheppey) *Kent*
11 E1
Minster (Thanet) *Kent* 11 F2
Minsterley 13 F1
Mintlaw 43 F3
Minworth 55 D2
Mirfield 25 F3
Mirfield 57 D2
Misterton 26 B4
Mitcham 52 D5
Mitcheldean 14 A3
Mobberley 20 A1
Mobberley 59 E4
Modbury 4 C3
Moelfre 18 B1
Moffat 34 B4
Mold 19 E2
Molescroft 27 D2
Mollington *Ches.* 58 A4
Mollinsburn 61 F1
Moniaive 34 A4
Monifieth 39 D3
Monimail 39 D4
Monken Hadley 52 D2
Monkokehampton 4 C1
Monks' Heath 59 F4
Monks Eleigh 17 D2
Monkton *T. & W.* 60 B2
Monkwearmouth 60 B3
Monmore Green 54 B2
Monmouth (Trefynwy) 7 F1
Monreith 28 B2
Montgomery (Trefaldwyn)
13 E1

Montrose 39 E2
Moodiesburn 61 E1
Moor Allerton 57 F1
Moore 58 C3
Moorends 26 B3
Moorgreen 56 B1
Morar 36 C1
Morden *Gt.Lon.* 52 D5
Mordon 60 A4
Morebattle 35 D3
Morecambe 24 C1
Morenish 38 A3
Moresby 29 E3
Moreton *Essex* 53 G1
Moreton *Mers.* 19 E1
Moreton-in-Marsh 14 C2
Moretonhampstead 5 D1
Morfa Nefyn 18 A3
Morley *Derbys.* 56 A1
Morley *W.Yorks.* 26 A3
Morley *W.Yorks.* 57 E2
Morley Green 59 F3
Morningside *Edin.* 61 E4
Morpeth 30 C1
Morriston 6 C1
Mortehoe 6 B3
Mortimer's Cross 13 F3
Mortlake 52 D4
Morton (Bourne) *Lincs.* 22 A3
Morton (Gainsborough) *Lincs.*
26 C4
Morton Bagot 55 D5
Morville 20 A4
Mosborough 26 A4
Mosborough 57 E4
Moscow 33 F3
Moseley *W.Mid.* 54 C3
Mossat 43 D4
Moss Bank 58 C2
Mossblown 33 E3
Mossend 61 F2
Mossley 25 E4
Mossley Hill 58 A3
Moss Nook 59 F3
Mosstodloch 42 C2
Motherwell 34 A2
Motherwell 61 F3
Mottingham 53 F4
Mottram St. Andrew 59 F4
Mouldsworth 58 C4
Moulsecoomb 10 B4
Moulton *Ches.* 59 D5
Moulton *Lincs.* 22 A3
Moulton *Suff.* 16 C1
Mountain Ash 7 E1
Mountbenger 34 C3
Mount Manisty 58 A4
Mountnessing 53 H2
**Mount Pleasant *Derbys.*
56 A1**
Mountsorrel 21 E3
Mow Cop 56 B3
Mowtie 39 F1
Moxley 54 B2
Moy 42 A3
Muchalls 39 F1
Much Wenlock 20 A4
Muirdrum 39 E3
Muirhead *Angus* 39 D3
Muirhead *N.Lan.* 61 E2
Muirkirk 33 F3
Muir of Fowlis 43 D4
Muir of Ord 41 F2
Mulbarton 23 E4
Mulben 42 C2
Mullion 3 E4
Mundesley 23 E2
Mundford 22 C4
Munlochy 42 A2
Murton 31 D2
Musbury 5 F1

Musselburgh 34 C1
Musselburgh 61 F4
Mustow Green 54 A4
Muthill 38 B4
Mybster 45 E2
Mytholmroyd 25 E3

N

Nailsea 7 F2
Nailsea 51 E4
Nailsworth 14 B3
Nairn 42 A2
Nantgarw 51 D1
Nantwich 20 A2
Nantyglo 7 E1
Narberth 6 A1
Narborough *Leics.* 21 D4
Narborough *Norf.* 22 C3
Nash *Newport* 51 D3
Nateby 30 B4
Navestock 53 G2
Navestock Side 53 G2
Nazeing 16 B4
Nazeing 53 F1
Neal's Green 55 F3
Near Sawrey 29 F4
Neasham 60 A5
Neath 6 C1
Necton 23 D4
Needham Market 17 D2
Needingworth 16 B1
Nefyn 18 A3
Neilston 33 F2
Nelson 25 E2
Nenthead 30 B2
Nerston 61 E3
Ness 58 A4
Neston 19 E1
Nether Alderley 59 F4
Nether Haugh 57 E3
Nether Langwith 21 D1
Netherley 39 F1
Nether Stowey 7 E3
Netherthorpe 57 F4
Netherton *Ches.* 58 C4
Netherton *Mers.* 58 A1
Netherton *W.Mid.* 54 B3
Nether Whitacre 55 E2
Nethy Bridge 42 B4
Netley 50 B2
Netley Marsh 50 A1
Nettlebed 15 E4
Nettleham 21 F1
New Abbey 29 D1
New Aberdour 43 E2
New Addington 10 B2
New Addington 53 E5
New Alresford 9 E2
Newark-on-Trent 21 E1
New Arley 55 E2
Newarthill 61 F3
New Ash Green 10 C2
New Ash Green 53 H5
New Barn 53 H5
New Barnet 52 D2
Newbiggin-by-the-Sea 31 D1
Newbigging 34 A2
Newbold Verdon 21 D3
Newborough 22 A4
Newbridge *Caerp.* 7 E1
Newbridge *Edin.* 61 D4
Newbridge *Hants.* 50 A1
New Brighton *Hants.* 50 B4
New Brighton *Mers.* 58 A2
Newburgh *Aber.* 43 F3
Newburgh *Fife* 39 D4
Newburn 30 C1
Newbury 9 E1
Newby *N.Yorks.* 60 C5

Newby Bridge 29 F4
New Byth 43 E2
Newcastle *Shrop.* 13 E2
Newcastle (Woolsington)
Airport 30 C1
Newcastle-under-Lyme
20 B2
**Newcastle-under-Lyme
56 B4**
Newcastle Emlyn 12 B4
Newcastleton 29 F1
Newcastle upon Tyne 30 C1
Newcastle upon Tyne 60 A2
Newchapel *Staffs.* 56 B3
Newchapel 61 F4
New Cumnock 33 F4
New Deer 43 E3
New Edlington 57 F3
New Eltham 53 F4
Newent 14 A2
New Farnley 57 E1
New Ferry 58 A3
Newfield *Dur.* 60 A3
New Galloway 28 C1
Newgate Street 53 E1
Newham *Gt.Lon.* 53 E3
New Hartley 60 B1
New Haw 52 B5
Newhouse 61 F2
Newick 10 B3
Newington 11 D2
New Invention *W.Mid.* 54 B1
New Leeds 43 F2
New Luce 28 A1
Newlyn 3 D3
Newmachar 43 E4
New Malden 52 D5
Newmarket *Suff.* 16 C1
Newmarket *W.Isles* 47 F2
Newmill 37 D2
New Mills 25 E4
Newmills 33 F3
New Mistley 17 E3
Newnham 14 A3
New Pitsligo 43 E2
Newport *Essex* 16 B2
Newport *High.* 45 E3
Newport *I.o.W.* 9 E4
Newport *Newport* 7 F2
Newport *Newport* 51 D3
Newport *Pembs.* 12 A4
Newport *Shrop.* 20 A1
Newport-on-Tay 39 D3
Newport Pagnell 15 F2
Newquay 3 E2
New Quay 12 B3
New Radnor 13 E3
New Romney 11 E3
New Rossington 26 B4
New Sawley 56 B2
New Scone 38 C3
New Silksworth 60 B3
Newton *Arg. & B.* 37 E4
Newton *Ches.* 58 C4
Newton (Bowland) *Lancs.*
25 D2
Newton-le-Willows *Mers.*
19 F1
**Newton-le-Willows *Mers.*
58 C2**
Newton Abbot 5 D2
Newton Aycliffe 31 D3
Newton Bewley 60 B4
Newton Burgoland 55 F1
Newton Ferrers 4 C3
Newtonhill 39 F1
Newton Mearns 33 F3
Newton Mearns 61 D3
Newtonmore 42 A4

Newton Poppleford 5 E1
Newton Regis 55 E1
Newton St. Cyres 5 D1
Newton Stewart 28 B1
**Newton under Roseberry
60 C5**
Newtown *Bucks.* 52 A1
Newtown *Hants.* 50 C1
Newtown *H. & W.* 14 A2
Newtown (Y Drenewydd)
Powys 13 E2
Newtown St. Boswells
35 D3
New Tredegar 7 E1
Newtyle 39 D3
New York *T. & W.* 60 B1
Neyland 6 A1
Niddrie 61 E4
Nine Ashes 53 G1
Ninfield 11 D4
Nisbet 35 D3
Nitshill 61 D2
Noak Hill 53 G2
**No Man's Heath *Warks.*
55 E1**
Norbiton 52 C5
Norchard 54 A5
Norham 35 E2
Norley 58 C4
Normanby *R. & C.* 60 C5
Normanton *Derbys.* 56 A2
Normanton *W.Yorks.* 26 A3
Normanton *W.Yorks.* 57 F2
Northallerton 31 D4
Northam *Devon* 6 B3
Northam *Hants.* 50 B1
Northampton 15 E1
North Anston 57 F4
Northaw 52 D1
North Baddesley 9 D2
North Ballachulish 37 E2
North Berwick 34 C1
North Boarhunt 50 A3
North Carlton *Notts.* 57 F4
North Cave 26 C2
North Cheriton 8 A2
Northchurch 52 A1
North Cowton 31 D4
North Cray 53 F4
North Duffield 26 B2
North Elmham 23 D3
North End *Hants.* 50 A4
North Ferriby 26 C3
Northfield *W.Mid.* 54 C4
Northfleet 10 C1
Northfleet 53 H4
North Grimston 26 C1
North Hayling 50 B4
North Hykeham 21 F1
Northill 16 A2
North Kessock 42 A3
Northleach 14 C3
North Leigh 15 D3
North Marden 50 C3
North Middleton 34 C2
North Molton 6 C4
North Mundham 50 C4
Northney 50 B4
North Ockendon 53 G3
Northolt 52 C3
North Ormesby 60 C4
Northowram 57 D2
North Queensferry 34 B1
North Rode 59 F4
North Shields 31 D1
North Shields 60 B2
North Somercotes 27 E4
North Stifford 53 H3
North Stoneham 50 B1
North Sunderland 35 F3
North Thoresby 27 E4

North Tidworth 9 D1
North Walsham 23 E2
North Weald Bassett 16 B4
North Weald Bassett 53 F1
Northwich 20 A1
Northwich 59 D4
Northwick 51 F3
North Wingfield 21 D1
Northwood *Gt.Lon.* 52 B2
Northwood *I.o.W.* 9 E3
Norton *Ches.* 58 C3
Norton *N.Yorks.* 26 C1
Norton *S.Yorks.* 57 D4
Norton *Stock.* 60 B4
Norton *Suff.* 17 D1
Norton *W.Mid.* 54 A3
**Norton-Juxta-Twycross
55 F1**
Norton Canes 20 B3
Norton Canes 54 C1
Norton Fitzwarren 7 E4
Norton Heath 53 H1
Norton in the Moors 56 B3
Norton Lindsey 55 E4
Norton Mandeville 53 G1
Norwich 23 E4
Norwich Airport 23 E3
Norwick 48 C1
Norwood Green 52 C4
Nottingham 21 D2
Nottingham 56 C1
Nuneaton 21 D4
Nuneaton 55 F2
Nunthorpe 60 C5
Nursling 50 A1
Nurton 54 A2
Nutbourne *W.Suss.* 50 B4
Nuthall 56 C1
Nuthurst *Warks.* 55 D4

O

Oadby 21 E4
Oakdale 7 E1
Oaken 54 A1
Oakengates 20 A3
Oakenshaw *W.Yorks.* 57 D2
Oakham 21 F3
Oakley *Bucks.* 15 E3
Oakley *Fife* 34 A1
Oakley *Hants.* 9 E1
Oakley Green 52 A4
Oban 37 D3
Occlestone Green 59 D5
Ochiltree 33 F3
Ockbrook 21 D2
Ockbrook 56 B2
Ockle 36 C2
Oddington 15 D3
Oddsta 48 C1
Odiham 9 F1
Odstone 55 F1
Offchurch 55 F5
Ogmore 7 D2
Ogmore Vale 7 D1
Okehampton 4 C1
Old Arley 55 E2
Old Basford 56 C1
Oldberrow 55 D5
Oldbury *Warks.* 55 F2
Oldbury *W.Mid.* 20 B4
Oldbury *W.Mid.* 54 B2
Old Colwyn 18 C1
Oldcotes 57 F4
Old Craighall 61 F4
Old Dailly 33 E4
Old Felixstowe 17 E2
Oldfield *H. & W.* 54 A5
Oldham 25 E4
Old Hill 54 B3
Oldland 8 A1
Old Leake 22 B2

Oldmeldrum 43 E3
Old Milverton 55 E5
Old Netley 50 B1
Old Swinford 54 B3
Old Windsor 52 A4
Olgrinmore 45 E2
Ollaberry 48 B2
Ollerton *Ches.* 59 E4
Ollerton *Notts.* 21 E1
Olney 15 F1
Olton 55 D3
Olveston 14 A4
Olveston 51 F3
Ombersley 14 B1
Ombersley 54 A5
Onchan 24 B3
Onich 37 E2
Onneley 56 A4
Orford *Ches.* 59 D2
Orford *Suff.* 17 F2
Ormesby 60 C4
Ormesby St. Margaret 23 F3
Ormiston 34 C1
Ormskirk 24 C3
Ormskirk 58 B1
Orpington 10 C2
Orpington 53 F5
Orrell 25 D3
Orrell 58 C1
Orsett 53 H3
Orton 30 A4
Orton-on-the-Hill 55 F1
Orton Longueville 22 A4
Oscroft 58 C5
Oskaig 40 B3
Osmaston *Derbys.* 56 A2
Ossett 26 A3
Ossett 57 E2
Osterley 52 C4
Oswaldkirk 26 B1
Oswaldtwistle 25 D3
Oswestry 19 E3
Otford 10 C2
Otley *Suff.* 17 E2
Otley *W.Yorks.* 25 F2
Otterburn 35 E4
Otter Ferry 33 D1
Ottershaw 52 B5
Otterswick 48 C2
Ottery St. Mary 5 E1
Oughtibridge 26 A4
Oughtibridge 57 D3
Oulton *Suff.* 23 F4
Oulton *W.Yorks.* 57 F2
Oundle 15 F4
Ouston *Dur.* 60 A3
Outwell 22 B4
Outwood *W.Yorks.* 57 F2
Over *Ches.* 59 D5
Over *S.Glos.* 51 F3
Overbister 49 F2
Over Peover 59 E4
Overpool 58 A4
Overseal 20 C3
Over Tabley 59 E3
Overton *Hants.* 9 E1
Overton *Wrex.* 19 F3
Overtown 34 A2
Over Wallop 9 D2
Over Whitacre 55 E2
Ower 50 A1
Oxenhope 25 F2
Oxford 15 D3
Oxley 54 B1
Oxnam 35 D3
Oxshott 10 A2
Oxshott 52 C5
Oxted 10 B2
Oxton *Bord.* 34 C2
Oxton *Mers.* 58 A3
Oykel Bridge 41 F1

P

Padbury 15 E2
Paddington 52 D3
Paddock Wood 11 D2
Padiham 25 E2
Padstow 3 F2
Paignton 5 D2
Painswick 14 B3
Paisley 33 F2
Palnackie 29 D2
Pandy 13 F4
Pangbourne 15 E4
Pant-y-dwr 13 D2
Papworth Everard 16 A1
Par 4 A3
Parbold 24 C3
Park Gate 50 C2
Parkgate S.Yorks. 57 E3
Park Street 52 C1
Partick 61 D2
Partington 25 D4
Partington 59 E2
Partney 22 B1
Parton 29 D3
Passingford Bridge 53 F2
Patchway 14 A4
Patchway 51 F3
Pateley Bridge 25 F1
Path of Condie 38 C4
Patna 33 E4
Patrick 24 A2
Patrington 27 E3
Patterdale 29 F3
Pattingham 54 A2
Paulton 8 A1
Paxton 35 E2
Peacehaven 10 B4
Peasedown St. John 8 B1
Pedmore 54 B3
Peebles 34 B2
Peel 24 A2
Pegswood 30 C1
Peinchorran 40 B3
Pelaw 60 A2
Pelsall 20 B3
Pelsall 54 C1
Pelton 60 A3
Pelynt 4 A3
Pembrey 6 B1
Pembridge 13 F3
Pembroke 12 B2
Pembroke Dock 12 B2
Pembury 10 C3
Pen-y-bont-fawr 19 D3
Penally 6 A1
Penarth 7 E2
Penarth 51 D2
Pencader 12 B4
Pencaitland 34 C1
Pencoed 7 D2
Pendeen 3 D3
Pendine 6 A1
Pendlebury 25 E4
Pendlebury 59 E1
Penge 53 E4
Penicuik 34 B2
Peninver 32 C3
Penistone 25 F4
Penketh 58 C3
Penkridge 20 B3
Penley 19 F3
Penmaenmawr 18 C1
Penn Bucks. 52 A2
Penn W.Mid. 54 A2
Penn Street 52 A2
Pennyghael 36 C3
Penpont 34 A4
Penrhiw-pal 12 B3
Penrhyn Bay 18 C1
Penrhyndeudraeth 18 B3

Penrith 30 A3
Penryn 3 F3
Penshaw 60 B3
Pensilva 4 B2
Pensnett 54 B3
Pentir 18 B2
Pentraeth 18 B1
Pentre 7 D1
Pentre-Poeth 51 E1
Pentrefoelas 18 C2
Pentwyn 51 E1
Pentyrch 51 D1
Penwortham 25 D3
Penybont 13 E3
Penygraig 7 D1
Penygroes 18 B2
Penywaun 7 D1
Penzance 3 D3
Peover Heath 59 E4
Perivale 52 C3
Perranporth 3 E2
Perry Barr 54 C2
Perry Street 53 H4
Pershore 14 B2
Perth 38 C3
Perton 54 A2
Peterborough 22 A4
Peterculter 43 E4
Peterhead 43 F3
Peterlee 31 D2
Petersfield 9 F2
Peterstone Wentlooge 51 E1
Petworth 10 A3
Pevensey 10 C4
Pewsey 8 C1
Piccotts End 52 B1
Pickerells 53 G1
Pickering 31 F4
Pickford Green 55 E3
Pickmere 59 D4
Picton Ches. 58 B4
Piddletrenthide 8 B3
Pierowall 49 E2
Pilgrims Hatch 16 B4
Pilgrims Hatch 53 G2
Pill 51 F4
Pilling 24 C2
Pilning 7 F2
Pilning 51 F3
Pimperne 8 B3
Pinchbeck 22 A3
Pinchinthorpe 60 C5
Pinhoe 5 D1
Pinley Green 55 E5
Pinner 52 C3
Pinner Green 52 C2
Pinwherry 28 A1
Pipe Gate 56 A4
Pirbright 9 F1
Pirnmill 32 C2
Pitagowan 38 B2
Pitlochry 38 B2
Pitmedden 43 E3
Pitscottie 39 D4
Pitt 9 E2
Pittentrail 42 A1
Pittenweem 39 E4
Plains 61 F2
Plean 34 A1
Pleasley 21 D1
Plumley 59 E4
Plumstead Gt.Lon. 53 F4
Plwmp 12 B3
Plymouth 4 C3
Plympton 4 C3
Plymstock 4 C3
Pocklington 26 C2
Polbeth 34 A2
Polegate 10 C4
Polesworth 20 C3
Polesworth 55 E1

Polloch 37 D2
Pollokshaws 61 D2
Polmont 34 A1
Polnoon 61 D3
Polperro 4 A3
Polwarth 35 D2
Pondersbridge 22 A4
Ponders End 53 E2
Pontardawe 6 C1
Pontardulais 6 C1
Pontefract 26 A3
Ponteland 30 C1
Pontesbury 13 F1
Pontlanfraith 7 E1
Pontrhydfendigaid 12 C3
Pontrilas 13 F4
Pontyberem 6 B1
Pontycymer 7 D1
Pontymister 51 E1
Pontypool 7 E1
Pontypridd 7 E1
Pooksgreen 50 A1
Pool 25 F2
Poole 8 C4
Poolewe 40 C1
Pooley Bridge 29 F3
Pool of Muckhart 38 C4
Poplar 53 E3
Porlock 7 D3
Port Appin 37 D3
Port Askaig 32 B1
Port Bannatyne 33 D2
Portbury 51 E4
Portchester 9 E3
Portchester 50 A4
Port Clarence 60 C4
Port Driseach 33 D1
Port Ellen 32 A2
Portencross 33 D2
Port Erin 24 A3
Portesham 8 A4
Port Eynon 6 B2
Port Glasgow 33 E1
Porth 7 D1
Porthcawl 7 D2
Port Henderson 40 C2
Porthleven 3 E4
Porthmadog 18 B3
Portishead 7 F2
Portishead 51 E4
Portknockie 43 D2
Portlethen 39 F1
Port Logan 28 A2
Portmahomack 42 B1
Portnacroish 37 D2
Portnahaven 32 A2
Portnalong 40 A3
Port nan Giúran 47 F2
Port nan Long 46 B1
Portnancon 44 B1
Port Nis 47 F1
Portobello 51 E1
Port of Menteith 38 A4
Portpatrick 28 A2
Portreath 3 E3
Portree 40 B3
Portsea 50 A4
Portskewett 51 F3
Portsmouth 9 E3
Portsmouth 50 A4
Portsoy 43 D2
Port St. Mary 24 A3
Port Sunlight 58 A3
Portswood 50 B1
Portway H. & W. 54 C4
Port William 28 B2
Potten End 52 B1
Potter's Cross 54 A3
Potterne 8 C1
Potters Bar 16 A4

Potters Bar 52 D1
Potters Crouch 52 C1
Potter Street 53 F1
Potton 16 A2
Poulton-le-Fylde 24 C2
Powburn 35 F3
Powick 14 B1
Powmill 38 C4
Poyle 52 B4
Poynton 25 E4
Pratt's Bottom 53 F5
Prees 19 F3
Preesall 24 C2
Prenton 58 A3
Prescot 19 F1
Prescot 58 B2
Prestatyn 19 D1
Prestbury Ches. 20 B1
Prestbury Glos. 14 B3
Presteigne 13 F3
Prestolee 59 E1
Preston Bord. 35 D2
Preston Dorset 8 B4
Preston E.Riding 27 D3
Preston Lancs. 25 D3
Preston T. & W. 60 B2
Preston Bagot 55 D5
Preston Brook 58 C3
Preston on the Hill 58 C3
Prestonpans 34 C1
Prestonpans 61 F4
Prestwich 25 E4
Prestwich 59 F1
Prestwick 33 E3
Prestwick Airport 33 E3
Prestwood 15 E3
Princes End 54 B2
Princes Risborough 15 E3
Princethorpe 15 D1
Princetown 4 C2
Probus 3 F3
Prudhoe 30 C2
Puddinglake 59 E5
Puddington Ches. 58 A4
Puddletown 8 B3
Pudsey 25 F2
Pudsey 57 E1
Pulborough 10 A3
Pumsaint 12 C3
Purbrook 50 A4
Purfleet 10 C3
Purfleet 53 G4
Puriton 7 E3
Purley 10 B2
Purley 53 E5
Purley on Thames 15 E4
Purton 14 C4
Putney 52 D4
Pwllheli 18 A3
Pye Corner Newport 51 D3
Pyle 7 D2

Q

Quarndon 56 A1
Quarry Bank 54 B3
Quarrybank 58 C5
Quarter 61 F3
Quedgeley 14 A3
Queenborough 11 D1
Queensbury 25 F3
Queensbury 57 D3
Queensferry 19 E2
Queensferry 58 A5
Queniborough 21 E3
Quernmore 25 D1
Queslett 54 C2
Quinton W.Mid. 54 B3

R

Raby 58 A4
Rackheath 23 E3
Radcliffe Gt.Man. 25 E3
Radcliffe Gt.Man. 59 E1
Radcliffe on Trent 21 E2
Radford W.Mid. 55 F3
Radford Semele 15 D1
Radford Semele 55 F5
Radlett 16 A4
Radlett 52 C1
Radstock 8 A1
Radway Green 56 A3
Radyr 51 D1
Rafford 42 B2
Raglan 7 F1
Rainford 24 C4
Rainford 58 B1
Rainham Gt.Lon. 53 G3
Rainhill 19 F1
Rainhill 58 B2
Rainhill Stoops 58 C2
Rainow 30 D3
Rainworth 21 E1
Rait 39 D3
Rampside 24 C1
Ramsbottom 25 E3
Ramsbury 14 C4
Ramsey Cambs. 16 A1
Ramsey I.o.M. 24 B2
Ramsey St. Mary's 22 A4
Ramsgate 11 F2
Ranskill 26 B3
Rastrick 57 D2
Ratcliffe Culey 55 F2
Rathillet 39 D3
Ratho 34 B1
Ratho 61 D4
Ratho Station 61 D4
Rattray 38 C3
Raunds 15 F1
Ravenfield 57 E3
Ravenglass 29 E4
Ravenshead 21 D2
Rawcliffe E.Riding 26 B3
Rawcliffe York 26 B2
Rawdon 57 E1
Rawmarsh 26 A4
Rawmarsh 57 E3
Rawtenstall 25 E3
Rawyards 61 F2
Rayleigh 11 D1
Rayne 16 C3
Reading 15 E4
Reay 45 D1
Redbourn 16 A3
Redbridge 53 F3
Redcar 31 E3
Redcastle 41 F3
Redcliff Bay 7 F2
Redcliff Bay 51 E4
Reddish 59 F2
Redditch 14 B1
Redditch 54 C5
Redford 39 E3
Red Hill Hants. 50 B3
Redhill Notts. 56 C1
Redhill Surr. 10 B2
Redland Bristol 51 F4
Redlynch 8 C2
Redmarshall 60 A4
Rednal W.Mid. 54 C4
Redpoint 40 C2
Red Roses 6 A1
Redruth 3 E3
Red Street 56 B3
Redwick Newport 51 E3
Redwick S.Glos. 51 F3
Reepham 23 E3
Reigate 10 B2

Reiss 45 F2
Renfrew 33 F2
Renfrew 61 D2
Rennington 35 F3
Repton 20 C3
Rescobie 39 E2
Resolven 7 D1
Reston 35 E2
Retford (East Retford) 21 E1
Reydon 17 F1
Rhayader 13 D2
Rhiconich 44 B2
Rhiwderin 51 E1
Rhondda 7 D1
Rhoose 7 E2
Rhos 6 C1
Rhos-on-Sea 18 C1
Rhosllanerchrugog 19 E2
Rhossili 6 B2
Rhu 33 E1
Rhuddlan 19 D1
Rhyl 19 D1
Rhymney 7 E1
Rhynie 43 D3
Ribchester 25 D2
Richings Park 52 B4
Richmond 30 C4
Richmond upon Thames 52 C4
Rickinghall 17 D1
Rickmansworth 10 A1
Rickmansworth 52 B2
Ridge *Herts.* **52 D1**
Ridge Lane 55 E2
Ridgeway 57 E4
Riding Mill 30 C2
Ridley 53 H5
Riggend 61 F2
Rigside 34 A3
Ringford 28 C2
Ringmer 10 C4
Ringwood 8 C3
Ripley *Derbys.* 21 D2
Ripley *N.Yorks.* 26 A1
Ripple 14 B2
Ripponden 25 F3
Risca 7 E1
Rishton 25 D3
Risley 21 D2
Risley 56 B2
Roade 15 E1
Roadside 45 E1
Roadside of Kinneff 39 F1
Roath 7 E2
Roath 51 E2
Roberton *Bord.* 34 C4
Roberton *S.Lan.* 34 A3
Roberttown 57 D2
Robin Hood *W.Yorks.* **57 F2**
Robin Hood's Bay 31 F4
Roby 58 B2
Roby Mill 58 C1
Rocester 20 C2
Rochdale 25 E3
Roche 4 A2
Rochester *Kent* 11 D2
Rochester *Nhumb.* 35 E4
Rochford 11 D1
Rock 14 A1
Rockcliffe 29 D2
Rock Ferry 58 A3
Rockingham 21 F4
Rode Heath 20 A1
Rode Heath 56 B3
Rodeheath 59 F5
Rodney Stoke 7 F3
Roehampton 52 D4
Rogart 45 D4
Rogate 9 F2
Rogerstone 7 E2

Rogerstone 51 E1
Roghadal 47 D4
Rogiet 51 E3
Roker 60 C3
Romanby 31 D4
Romannobridge 34 B2
Romford *Gt.Lon.* 10 C1
Romford *Gt.Lon.* **53 G2**
Romney Street 53 G5
Romsey 9 D2
Romsley *H. & W.* 20 B4
Romsley *H. & W.* **54 B3**
Ropley 9 E2
Ropsley 21 F2
Rosedale Abbey 31 E4
Rosehearty 43 F2
Rosemarkie 42 A2
Rosewell 34 B2
Roshven 37 D1
Roskhill 40 A3
Roslin 34 B2
Ross-on-Wye 14 A2
Rossett 19 E2
Rossington 26 B4
Rostherne 59 E3
Rothbury 35 E4
Rotherfield 10 C3
Rotherham 26 A4
Rotherham 57 E3
Rothes 42 C3
Rothesay 33 D2
Rothiesholm 49 F3
Rothley 21 E3
Rothwell *Nhants.* 21 E4
Rothwell *W.Yorks.* 26 A3
Rothwell *W.Yorks.* **57 F2**
Rottingdean 10 B4
Roughley 55 D2
Roughton 23 E2
Roundhay 57 F1
Roundway 8 C1
Rowde 8 C1
Rowington 55 E5
Rowington Green 55 E4
Rowland's Castle 50 B3
Rowlands Gill 30 C2
Rowley Regis 54 B3
Rowner 50 C2
Rowney Green 54 C4
Rownhams 50 A1
Rowton *Ches.* **58 B5**
Row Town 52 B5
Roxwell 53 H1
Royal Leamington Spa 14 C1
Royal Leamington Spa **55 F5**
Royal Tunbridge Wells 10 C3
Roybridge 37 F1
Roydon 17 D1
Roydon Hamlet 53 F1
Royston *Herts.* 16 B2
Royston *S.Yorks.* 26 A3
Royton 25 E3
Ruabon 19 E3
Ruardean 14 A3
Rubery 54 B4
Ruddington 21 E2
Ruddington 56 C2
Rudgwick 10 A3
Rudheath 59 D4
Rudry 51 D1
Rudston 27 D1
Rudyard 56 C3
Rufford 24 C3
Rugby 15 D1
Rugeley 20 B3
Ruislip 52 B3
Rumney 7 E2
Rumney 51 E2
Runcorn 19 F1
Runcorn 25 D4

Runcorn 58 C3
Runcton 50 C4
Runwell 11 D1
Rushall *W.Mid.* 20 B4
Rushall *W.Mid.* **54 C1**
Rushden 15 F1
Rush Green 53 G3
Rushmere St. Andrew 17 E2
Rushock 54 A4
Rusholm 59 F2
Rushton *Ches.* **58 C5**
Ruskington 22 A2
Ruspidge 14 A3
Rustington 10 A4
Rutherend 61 E3
Rutherglen 33 F2
Rutherglen 61 E2
Ruthin 19 D2
Ruyton-XI-Towns 19 F3
Ryde 11 E3
Rye 11 E3
Rye Park 53 E1
Ryhall 21 F3
Ryhope 60 C3
Ryton-on-Dunsmore 55 F4

S

Sacriston 30 C2
Sadberge 60 A5
Saddell 32 C3
Saffron Walden 16 B2
Saham Toney 23 D4
Saighdinis 46 B1
St. Abbs 35 E1
St. Agnes 3 E3
St. Albans 16 A3
St. Albans 52 C1
St. Andrews 39 E4
St. Andrews Major 51 D2
St. Asaph (Llanelwy) 19 D1
St. Athan 7 D2
St. Austell 4 A3
St. Bees 29 D3
St. Briavels 14 A3
St. Brides Major 7 D2
St. Brides Netherwent 51 E3
St. Brides Wentlooge 51 E1
St. Buryan 3 D4
St. Clears 12 A4
St. Columb Major 3 F2
St. Combs 43 F2
St. Cyrus 39 F2
St. David's 12 A1
St. Day 3 E3
St. Dennis 3 F2
St. Dogmaels 12 A3
St. Endellion 4 A2
St. Enoder 3 F2
St. Fagans 51 D2
St. Fergus 43 F2
St. Fillans 38 A3
St. Germans 4 B3
St. Helens *Mers.* 25 D4
St. Helens *Mers.* **58 C2**
St. Ishmael 6 B1
St. Ive 4 B2
St. Ives *Cambs.* 16 A1
St. Ives *Cornw.* 3 D3
St. John's Chapel 30 B2
St. John's Town of Dalry 28 C1
St. Just 3 D3
St. Just in Roseland 3 F3
St. Keverne 3 F4
St. Leonards 8 C3
St. Lythans 51 D2
St. Margaret's at Cliffe 11 F2
St. Margaret's Hope 49 E4
St. Martin's 19 E3
St. Mary Bourne 9 D1

St. Mary Cray 53 F5
St. Mary's 49 E3
St. Mary's Bay 11 E3
St. Mawes 3 F3
St. Mellons 51 E1
St. Merryn 3 E1
St. Mellons 51 E1
St. Monans 39 E4
St. Neots 16 A1
St. Osyth 17 E3
St. Paul's Cray 53 F5
St. Peter's 11 F1
St. Stephen 3 F2
St. Stephens *Herts.* **52 C1**
St. Teath 4 A2
Salcombe 4 C3
Sale 25 E4
Sale 59 E2
Salen *Arg. & B.* 36 C3
Salen *High.* 37 D2
Salford *Gt.Man.* 25 E4
Salford *Gt.Man.* **59 F2**
Salfords 10 B2
Salhouse 23 E3
Saline 34 A1
Salisbury 8 C2
Salsburgh 34 A2
Saltash 4 B3
Saltburn-by-the-Sea 31 E3
Saltcoats 33 E3
Saltdean 10 B4
Salterswall 59 D5
Saltford 8 A1
Salt Hill 52 A4
Saltley 54 C3
Saltney 19 E2
Saltney 58 A5
Sanaigmore 32 A1
Sandbach 20 A1
Sanderstead 53 E5
Sandgarth 49 E3
Sandhead 28 A2
Sandhurst 9 F1
Sandiacre 21 D2
Sandiacre 56 B2
Sandiway 59 D4
Sandness 48 A3
Sandown 9 E4
Sandplace 4 B3
Sandridge 16 A3
Sandsend 31 F3
Sandwich 11 F2
Sandwick 48 B4
Sandy 16 A2
Sandycroft 58 A5
Sandygate 24 B2
Sandy Lane *W.Yorks.* **57 D1**
Sanquhar 34 A4
Sapcote 21 D4
Sarisbury 50 C2
Sarratt 52 B2
Sarre 11 F2
Satley 30 C2
Saughall 58 A5
Saundersfoot 6 A1
Sawbridgeworth 16 B3
Sawley *Derbys.* **56 B2**
Sawston 16 B2
Sawtry 16 A1
Saxilby 21 F1
Saxmundham 17 F1
Saxthorpe 23 E3
Scalasaig 36 B4
Scalby 31 F4
Scalloway 48 B3
Scampton 21 F1
Scapa 49 E3
Scarborough 31 F4
Scarcliffe 21 D1
Scarinish 36 A3
Scarisbrick 24 C3
Scarth Hill 58 B1

Scholar Green 56 B3
Scholes *W.Yorks.* **57 F1**
Scleddau 12 B1
Scole 17 E1
Sconser 40 B3
Scorton 30 C4
Scotch Corner 30 C4
Scotter 26 C4
Scotton 30 C4
Scourie 44 A2
Scousburgh 48 B4
Scrabster 45 E1
Scraptoft 21 E3
Scremerston 35 E2
Scunthorpe 26 C3
Seacroft *W.Yorks.* **57 F1**
Seaford 10 C4
Seaforth 58 A2
Seaham 31 D2
Seahouses 35 F3
Sealand 58 A5
Seamer 27 C1
Seamer *N.Yorks.* **60 B5**
Seascale 29 E4
Seaton *Cumb.* 29 E3
Seaton *Devon* 5 F1
Seaton *Nhumb.* **60 B1**
Seaton Burn 60 A1
Seaton Delaval 31 D1
Seaton Delaval 60 B1
Seaton Sluice 31 D1
Seaton Sluice 60 B1
Seckington 55 E1
Sedbergh 30 A4
Sedgebrook 21 F2
Sedgefield 31 D3
Sedgefield 60 A4
Sedgley 20 B4
Sedgley 54 C3
Seend 8 B1
Seer Green 52 A2
Sefton 58 A1
Seghill 31 D1
Seghill 60 A1
Seighford 20 B3
Seisdon 54 A2
Selattyn 19 E3
Selby 26 B3
Selkirk 34 C3
Sellafield 29 E4
Sellafirth 48 C1
Sellindge 11 E3
Selly Oak 54 C3
Selsdon 53 E5
Selsey 9 F4
Selston 21 D2
Send 10 A2
Sennen 3 D4
Sennybridge 13 D4
Setley 50 A2
Setter 48 B3
Settle 25 E1
Seven Kings 53 F3
Sevenoaks 10 C2
Seven Sisters 7 D1
Severn Beach 7 F2
Severn Beach 51 F3
Sewardstone 53 E2
Sgiogarstaigh 47 F1
Shackerley 54 A1
Shackerstone 55 F1
Shaftesbury 8 B2
Shalfleet 9 D4
Shalford 10 A2
Shanklin 9 E4
Shap 30 A3
Shardlow 56 B2
Shareshill 54 B1
Sharpness 14 A3
Shavington 20 A2

Shaw 25 E3
Shedfield 50 C1
Sheepway 51 E4
Sheepy Magna 55 F1
Sheepy Parva 55 F1
Sheering 16 B3
Sheerness 11 D1
Sheffield 26 A4
Sheffield 57 D4
Shefford 16 A2
Sheldon *W.Mid.* **55 D3**
Shelf 25 F3
Shelf 57 D2
Shelfield 54 C1
Shelley *Essex* 53 G1
Shellow Bowells 53 H1
Shenfield 53 H2
Shenley 52 C1
Shenleybury 52 C1
Shenstone *H. & W.* **54 A4**
Shenstone *Staffs.* 20 C3
Shenstone *Staffs.* **55 D1**
Shenstone Woodend 55 D1
Shenton 55 F1
Shepley 25 F3
Shepperton 10 A2
Shepperton 52 B5
Shepshed 21 D3
Shepton Mallet 8 A2
Sherborne 8 A3
Sherborne St. John 9 E1
Sherburn 31 D2
Sherburn in Elmet 26 A2
Shere 10 A2
Sheriffhales 20 A3
Sheriff Hutton 26 B1
Sheringham 23 E2
Sherston 14 B4
Shettleston 61 E2
Shevington 25 D3
Shevington 58 C1
Shiel Bridge 41 D4
Shieldaig 40 C2
Shieldhill 34 A1
Shifnal 20 A3
Shilbottle 35 F4
Shildon 30 C3
Shiney Row 60 B3
Shinfield 9 F1
Shinness Lodge 44 C3
Shiplake 15 E4
Shipley *Shrop.* **54 A2**
Shipley *W.Yorks.* 25 F2
Shipley *W.Yorks.* **57 D1**
Shipston on Stour 14 C2
Shipton *N.Yorks.* 26 B1
Shipton *Shrop.* 20 A4
Shipton-under-Wychwood
  14 C3
Shirebrook 21 D1
Shirehampton 51 F4
Shiremoor 31 D1
Shiremoor 60 B1
Shirenewton 7 F1
Shire Oak 54 C1
Shireoaks 57 F4
Shirland 21 D1
Shirley *Gt.Lon.* **53 E5**
Shirley *Hants.* 50 B1
Shirley *W.Mid.* **55 D4**
Shirrell Heath 50 C1
Sholing 50 B1
Shooter's Hill 53 F4
Shoreditch 53 E3
Shoreham *Kent* 10 C2
Shoreham *Kent* **53 F5**
Shoreham-by-Sea 10 B4
Short Heath *W.Mid.* **54 C2**
Shotley Gate 17 E2
Shottlegate 56 A1

Shotton *Flint.* 19 E2
Shotton *Flint.* **58 A5**
Shotts 34 A2
Shotwick 58 A4
Shrawley 54 A5
Shrewley 55 E5
Shrewsbury 13 F1
Shrewton 8 C2
Shustoke 55 E2
Shuttington 55 E1
Siabost 47 E1
Sible Hedingham 16 C2
Sibsey 22 B2
Sibson *Leics.* **55 F1**
Sidbury 5 E1
Sidcup 10 C1
Sidcup 53 F4
Siddington *Ches.* 59 F4
Sidford 5 E1
Sidley 11 D4
Sidmouth 5 E1
Sigglesthorne 27 D2
Sileby 21 E3
Silksworth 60 B3
Silloth 29 E2
Silsden 25 F2
Silverdale *Lancs.* 24 C1
Silverdale *Staffs.* **56 B4**
Silverstone 15 E2
Silverton 5 D1
Simonsbath 6 C3
Singleton *W.Suss.* **50 C3**
Singlewell or Ifield 53 H4
Sipson 52 B4
Sittingbourne 11 D2
Siulaisiadar 47 F2
Skaill (East Coast) *Ork.* 49 F3
Skaill (West Coast) *Ork.* 49 D3
Skaw 48 E2
Skegness 22 B1
Skelmersdale 24 C3
Skelmersdale 58 B1
Skelmorlie 33 E2
Skelton 31 E3
Skelwick 49 E2
Skenfrith 13 F4
Skerray 44 B2
Skipness 32 C2
Skipsea 27 D2
Skipton 25 E2
Slade Green 53 G4
Slaidburn 25 D2
Slaithwaite 25 F3
Slamannan 34 A1
Slattocks 59 F1
Sleaford 21 F2
Sledmere 26 C1
Sleights 11 E2
Sligachan 40 B3
Slinfold 10 A3
Slough 10 A1
Slough 52 A4
Smailholm 35 D3
Smalley 21 D2
Smalley 56 B1
Smallthorne 56 B4
Smeeth 11 E3
Smethwick 20 B4
Smethwick 54 C3
Smithy Green 59 E4
Smug Oak 52 C1
Snaith 26 B3
Snarestone 55 F1
Snettisham 22 C3
Snitterfield 14 C1
Snodland 11 D2
Soberton 50 A3
Soberton Heath 50 A3
Soham 16 B1

Solas 46 B1
Sole Street *Kent* **53 H5**
Solihull 20 C4
Solihull 55 D4
Solihull Lodge 54 C4
Solva 12 A1
Somercotes 21 D2
Somersham 16 B1
Somerton 7 F4
Sompting 10 B4
Sonning Common 15 E4
Sorbie 28 B2
Sorisdale 36 B2
Sorn 33 F2
Southall 52 C4
Southam 15 D1
Southampton 9 E3
Southampton 50 B1
Southampton Airport 9 D3
Southampton Airport 50 B1
South Anston 26 B4
South Anston 57 F4
South Bank 31 E3
South Bank 60 C4
South Beddington 52 D5
South Benfleet 11 D1
Southborough 10 C3
Southbourne *W.Suss.* 9 F3
Southbourne *W.Suss.* **50 B4**
South Brent 4 C2
South Cave 26 C3
South Chard 5 F1
South Darenth 53 G5
Southdean 35 D4
Southend *Arg. & B.* 32 C4
Southend-on-Sea 11 D1
Southery 22 C4
Southfleet 53 H4
Southgate *Gt.Lon.* 10 B1
Southgate *Gt.Lon.* **52 D2**
South Harting 9 F2
South Harting 50 B3
South Hetton 31 D2
South Hornchurch 53 G3
South Hylton 60 B3
South Kelsey 27 D4
South Kirkby 26 A3
South Leverton 26 C4
South Lopham 17 D1
South Mimms 52 D1
Southminster 17 D4
South Molton 6 C4
South Mundham 50 C4
South Normanton 21 D2
South Norwood 53 E5
South Ockendon 10 C1
South Ockendon 53 G3
Southowram 57 D2
South Oxhey 10 A1
South Oxhey 52 C2
South Petherton 7 F4
Southport 24 C3
South Queensferry 34 B1
South Queensferry 61 D4
South Shields 31 D1
South Shields 60 B2
South Skirlaugh 27 D2
South Street *Kent* **53 H5**
Southwark 53 E4
South Weald 53 G2
Southwell 21 E2
Southwick *Hants.* **50 A4**
Southwick *T. & W.* **60 B3**
Southwick *Wilts.* 8 B1
Southwold 17 F1
South Woodham Ferrers
  16 C4
South Wootton 22 C3
South Yardley 55 D3
Sowerby Bridge 25 F3
Spalding 22 A3

Spean Bridge 37 F1
Speen 9 D1
Speke 58 B3
Spennymoor 31 D3
Spey Bay 42 C2
Spilsby 22 B1
Spinningdale 42 A1
Spital *Berks.* **52 A4**
Spitalbrook 53 E1
Spittal 45 E2
Spittal of Glenshee 38 C2
Spixworth 23 E3
Spofforth 26 A2
Spondon 56 B2
Springburn 61 E2
Springfield *W.Mid.* **54 C3**
Springholm 29 D1
Springside 33 E3
Springwell 60 A3
Sproatley 27 D2
Sproston Green 59 E5
Sprowston 23 E3
Stadhampton 15 E3
Stadhlaigearraidh 46 A2
Staffin 40 B2
Stafford 20 B3
Staindrop 30 C3
Staines 10 A1
Staines 52 B4
Stainforth 25 E1
Stainforth 26 B3
Stainton *S.Yorks.* **57 F3**
Stainton *Stock.* **60 B5**
Staintondale 31 F4
Stalbridge 8 B3
Stalham 23 F3
Stalling Busk 30 B4
Stalybridge 25 F4
Stamford 21 F3
Stamfordham 30 C1
Stand 61 F2
Standeford 54 B1
Standish 25 D3
Standon 16 B3
Stane 34 A2
Stanford-le-Hope 11 D1
Stanford Rivers 53 G1
Stanhoe 22 C2
Stanhope 30 B2
Stanley *Derbys.* **56 B1**
Stanley *Dur.* 30 C2
Stanley *P. & K.* 38 C3
Stanley *Staffs.* **56 C3**
Stanley *W.Yorks.* 26 A3
Stanley *W.Yorks.* **57 F2**
Stanley Common 56 B1
Stanmore *Gt.Lon.* **52 C2**
Stannington *Nhumb.* 30 C1
Stannington *S.Yorks.* **57 D4**
Stansted 53 H5
Stansted Airport 16 B3
Stansted Mountfitchet 16 B3
Stanton 17 D1
Stanton by Dale 56 B2
Stanway 17 D3
Stanwell 52 B4
Stanwell Moor 52 B4
Stapleford *Notts.* 21 D2
Stapleford *Notts.* **56 B2**
Stapleford Abbotts 53 F2
Stapleford Tawney 53 G2
Staplehurst 11 D2
Stapleton *Bristol* **51 F4**
Starcross 5 D2
Startforth 30 C3
Statham 59 D3
Staunton 14 A2
Staveley 21 D1
Staxton 27 D1
Steeple Claydon 15 E2
Steeton 25 F2

Stenhousemuir 34 A1
Stenness 48 A2
Stenton 35 D1
Stepney 53 E3
Stepps 61 E2
Stevenage 16 A3
Stevenston 33 E3
Stewarton 33 E2
Steyning 10 B4
Stibb Cross 6 B4
Stichill 35 D3
Stickney 22 B2
Stillington *N.Yorks.* 26 B1
Stillington *Stock.* **60 A4**
Stilton 22 A4
Stirchley *W.Mid.* **54 C3**
Stirling 34 A1
Stivichall 55 F4
Stoak 58 B4
Stobo 34 B3
Stock 16 C4
Stockbridge 9 D2
Stockingford 55 F2
Stockport 25 F4
Stockport 59 F3
Stocksbridge 26 A4
Stocksfield 30 C2
Stockton-on-Tees 31 D3
Stockton-on-Tees 60 B4
Stockton Heath 19 F1
Stockton Heath 59 D3
Stoer 44 A3
Stoke *Hants.* **50 B4**
Stoke *W.Mid.* **55 F4**
Stoke-by-Nayland 17 D2
Stoke-on-Trent 20 B2
Stoke-on-Trent 56 B4
Stoke Albany 21 E4
Stoke Ash 17 E1
Stoke Golding 55 F2
Stoke Holy Cross 23 E4
Stoke Mandeville 15 F3
Stokenchurch 15 E4
Stoke Newington 53 E3
Stokenham 5 D3
Stoke Poges 10 A1
Stoke Poges 52 A4
Stoke Prior *H. & W.* 14 B1
Stoke Prior *H. & W.* **54 B5**
Stokesay 13 F2
Stokesley 31 E4
Stondon Massey 53 G1
Stone *Glos.* 14 A4
Stone *H. & W.* **54 A4**
Stone *Kent* 10 C1
Stone *Kent* **53 G4**
Stone *Staffs.* 20 B2
Stonebridge *Warks.* **55 E3**
Stonefield *S.Lan.* **61 E3**
Stonehaven 39 F1
Stonehouse *Glos.* 14 A3
Stonehouse *S.Lan.* 34 A2
Stoneleigh 55 F4
Stoneykirk 28 A3
Stonnall 54 C1
Stony Stratford 15 E2
Storeton 58 A3
Stornoway 47 F2
Storrington 10 A4
Stotfold 16 A2
Stoughton *W.Suss.* **50 C3**
Stourbridge 20 B4
Stourbridge 54 A3
Stourport-on-Severn 14 A1
Stourport-on-Severn 54 A4
Stourton *Staffs.* **54 A3**
Stow 34 C2
Stow-on-the-Wold 14 C2
Stowmarket 17 D2
Strachan 39 E1
Strachur 37 E4

Stradbroke 17 E1
Stradishall 16 C2
Stradsett 22 C4
Straloch 38 C2
Stranraer 28 A2
Stratford-upon-Avon 14 C1
Strathaven 33 F2
Strathblane 33 F1
Strathdon 42 C4
Strathmiglo 38 C4
Strathpeffer 41 F2
Strathy 45 D1
Strathyre 38 A4
Stratton 4 B1
Stratton St. Margaret 14 C4
Streatham 52 D4
Streatley 15 E4
Street 7 F4
Streetly 54 C2
Strensall 26 B1
Stretford 25 E4
Stretford 59 E2
Stretham 16 B1
Strettington 50 C4
Stretton (Burton upon Trent)
Staffs. 20 C3
Stretton (Warrington) *Ches.*
59 D3
Strichen 43 F2
Stromeferry 40 C3
Stromness 49 D3
Stronachlachar 37 F4
Strone 33 E1
Strontian 37 D2
Stroud 14 B3
Stuartfield 43 F3
Stubbington 50 C2
Studley *Warks.* 14 C1
Studley *Warks.* **54 C5**
Studley Common 54 C5
Sturminster Newton 8 B3
Sturry 11 E2
Sturton le Steeple 26 C4
Styal 59 F3
Sudbrook *Mon.* **51 F3**
Sudbury *Derbys.* 20 C2
Sudbury *Gt.Lon.* **52 C3**
Sudbury *Suff.* 17 D2
Sully 7 E2
Summer Bridge 25 F1
Summerleaze 51 E3
Sunbury 10 A1
Sunbury 52 C5
Sunderland 31 D2
Sunderland 60 B3
Sunningdale 52 A5
Sunninghill 9 F1
Sunninghill 52 A5
Sunniside *T. & W.* **60 A3**
Surbiton 52 C5
Surfleet 22 A3
Sutterton 22 A3
Sutton *Gt.Lon.* **52 D5**
Sutton (Ely) *Cambs.* 16 B1
Sutton at Hone 53 G4
Sutton Bridge 22 B3
Sutton Coldfield 20 C4
Sutton Coldfield 55 D2
Sutton Courtenay 15 D4
Sutton in Ashfield 21 D1
Sutton Leach 58 C2
Sutton on Trent 21 E1
Sutton Valence 11 D2
Sutton Weaver 58 C4
Swadlincote 20 C3
Swaffham 22 C4
Swalwell 60 A2
Swanage 8 C4
Swanland 26 C3
Swanley 10 C2

Swanley 53 G5
Swanmore 50 C1
Swanscombe 10 C1
Swanscombe 53 H4
Swansea 6 C1
Swanton Morley 23 D3
Swanwick *Hants.* **50 C2**
Sway 9 D3
Swaythling 50 B1
Swettenham 59 F5
Swillington 57 F1
Swindon *Glos.* 14 B2
Swindon *Staffs.* **54 A2**
Swindon *Wilts.* 14 C4
Swinefleet 26 C3
Swinton *Bord.* 35 E2
Swinton *Gt.Man.* **59 E1**
Swinton *S.Yorks.* 26 A4
Swinton *S.Yorks.* **57 E3**
Sworton Heath 59 D3
Sydenham *Gt.Lon.* **53 E4**
Symbister 48 C3
Symington *S.Ayr.* 33 E3
Symington *S.Lan.* 34 A3
Synod Inn 12 B3
Syre 44 C2
Syston 21 E3
Sytchampton 54 A5

T

Tabost 47 F1
Tadcaster 26 A2
Tadley 9 E1
Taffs Well 7 E2
Taffs Well 51 D1
Tain 42 A1
Takeley 16 B3
Talgarreg 12 B3
Talgarth 13 E4
Taliesin 12 C2
Talisker 40 A3
Talke 56 B3
Talladale 41 D2
Tamworth 20 C3
Tamworth 55 E1
Tannadice 39 E2
Tannochside 61 F2
Tansley 21 D1
Tanton 60 C5
Tanworth in Arden 55 D4
Taobh Tuath 47 D3
Tarbert (Jura) *Arg. & B.* 32 B1
Tarbert (Kintyre) *Arg. & B.*
32 C2
Tarbet 37 F4
Tarbolton 33 F3
Tardebigge 54 B5
Tarfside 39 E1
Tarleton 24 C3
Tarporley 19 F2
Tarporley 58 C5
Tarrel 42 B1
Tarves 43 E3
Tarvin 19 F2
Tarvin 58 B5
Tarvin Sands 58 B5
Tattershall 22 A2
Taunton 7 E4
Taverham 23 E3
Tavistock 4 C2
Tayinloan 32 C2
Taynuilt 37 E3
Tayport 39 D3
Tayvallich 32 C1
Team Valley 60 A2
Teangue 40 C4
Tebay 30 A4
Teddington *Gt.Lon.* **52 C4**
Tees-side Airport 31 D3

Tees-side Airport 60 A5
Teignmouth 5 D2
Telford 20 A3
Temple Bar 12 B3
Temple Sowerby 30 A3
Templeton 6 A1
Tenbury Wells 14 A1
Tenby 6 A1
Tenterden 11 D3
Terrington 26 B1
Terrington St. Clement 22 B3
Testwood 50 A1
Tetbury 14 B4
Tetford 22 A1
Tetney 27 E4
Tettenhall 54 A1
Tettenhall Wood 54 A2
Teviothead 34 C4
Tewkesbury 14 B2
Teynham 11 E2
Thame 15 E3
Thames Ditton 52 C5
Thamesmead 53 F3
Thatcham 9 E1
Thatto Heath 58 C2
Thaxted 16 C3
Theale 15 E4
The Bratch 54 A2
The Burf 54 A5
Thelwall 59 D3
The Mumbles 6 C2
The Stocks 11 D3
Thetford 23 D4
The Wrythe 52 D5
Theydon Bois 53 F2
Thong 53 H4
Thornaby-on-Tees 31 D3
Thornaby-on-Tees 60 B5
Thornbury 14 A4
Thorne 26 B3
Thornes 54 C1
Thorney *Bucks.* **52 B4**
Thorney *Cambs.* 22 A4
Thorngumbald 27 D3
Thornhill *Cardiff* **51 D1**
Thornhill *D. & G.* 34 A4
Thornhill *Hants.* **50 B1**
Thornhill *Stir.* 38 A4
Thornley 31 D2
Thornliebank 61 D3
Thornton *Fife* 39 D4
Thornton *Lancs.* 24 C2
Thornton *Mers.* 24 C4
Thornton *Mers.* **58 A1**
Thornton *Stock.* **60 B5**
Thornton *W.Yorks.* **57 D1**
Thornton-le-Moors 58 B4
Thorntonhall 61 D3
Thornton Hough 58 A3
Thornwood Common 53 F1
Thorpe *Surr.* **52 B5**
Thorpe-le-Soken 17 E3
Thorpe Constantine 55 E1
Thorpe Hesley 57 D3
Thorpe Larches 60 A4
Thorpe Market 23 E2
Thorpeness 17 F1
Thorpe on the Hill *Lincs.* 21 F1
Thorpe on the Hill *W.Yorks.*
57 F2
Thorpe Salvin 57 D1
Thorpe St. Andrew 23 E4
Thorpe Thewles 60 A4
Thrapston 21 F4
Threlkeld 29 F3
Threshers Bush 53 F1
Threshfield 25 E1
Thropton 35 E4
Thrumpton 56 C2
Thrumster 45 F2
Thrupp 14 B3

Thrybergh 26 A4
Thrybergh 57 E3
Thulston 56 B2
Thundersley 11 D1
Thurcroft 26 A4
Thurcroft 57 F4
Thurlby 22 A3
Thurmaston 21 E3
Thurnscoe 26 A4
Thursby 29 F2
Thurso 45 E1
Thurton 23 E4
Thwaite 30 B4
Tibbermore 38 C3
Tibshelf 21 D1
Ticehurst 11 D3
Tickenham 51 E4
Tickhill 26 B4
Tickhill 57 F3
Ticknall 21 D3
Tidenham 14 A4
Tideswell 20 C1
Tighnabruaich 33 D1
Tilbury 10 C1
Tilbury 53 H4
Tile Cross 55 D3
Tile Hill 55 E4
Tilehurst 15 E4
Tillicoultry 38 B4
Tillyfourie 43 D4
Tilston 19 F2
Timbersbrook 59 F5
Timperley 59 E3
Timsbury 8 A1
Timsgearraidh 47 D2
Tingewick 15 E2
Tingley 57 E2
Tingwall 49 E3
Tinshill 57 E1
Tinsley 57 E3
Tintagel 4 A1
Tintern Parva 7 F1
Tipton 54 B2
Tiptree 17 D3
Tisbury 8 B2
Titchfield 50 C2
Tiverton 7 D4
Toab 48 B4
Tobermory 36 C2
Toberonochy 37 D4
Toddington *Beds.* 15 F2
Toddington *Glos.* 14 B2
Todmorden 25 E3
Todwick 57 E4
Toft 48 B2
Togston 35 F4
Tolastadh a'Chaolais 47 E2
Tolastadh Ùr w 47 F1
Tollcross 61 E2
Tollesbury 17 D3
Tollesby 60 C5
Tolleshunt D'Arcy 17 D3
Toll of Birness 43 F3
Tolworth 52 C5
Tomatin 42 A3
Tomich 42 A2
Tomintoul 42 C4
Tomnavoulin 42 C3
Tonbridge 10 C2
Tongland 28 C2
Tong Street 57 D1
Tongue 44 C2
Tongwynlais 51 D1
Tonna 6 C1
Tonypandy 7 D1
Tonyrefail 7 D2
Toothill 50 A1
Toot Hill 53 G1
Topcliffe 26 A1
Topsham 5 D1
Tore 41 F2

Tormore 32 C3
Torphichen 34 A1
Torphins 43 D4
Torpoint 4 B3
Torquay 5 D2
Torrance 33 F1
Torrance *E.Dun.* **61 E1**
Torrance *S.Lan.* **61 E3**
Torridon 41 D2
Torrin 40 B4
Torthorwald 29 E1
Torver 29 F4
Toscaig 40 C3
Tosside 25 E2
Totland 9 D4
Totley 57 D4
Totnes 5 D2
Toton 56 C2
Tottenham 53 E2
Totteridge 52 D2
Tottington 25 E3
Totton 9 D3
Totton 50 A1
Towcester 15 E2
Tower Hamlets 53 E3
Tow Law 30 C2
Town Green 58 B1
Townhead of Greenlaw 29 D1
Towyn 19 D1
Trafford Park 59 E2
Tranent 34 C1
Trawsfynydd 18 C3
Trecastle 13 D4
Tredegar 7 E1
Tredington 14 C2
Treeton 26 A4
Treeton 57 E4
Trefeglwys 13 D2
Treforest Ind. Est. 51 D1
Trefriw 18 C2
Tregaron 12 C3
Tregony 3 F3
Tregynon 13 E1
Treharris 7 E1
Treherbert 7 D1
Trelech 12 A4
Trelleck 7 F1
Tremadog 18 B3
Trenance 3 F2
Trentham 56 B4
Trescott 54 A2
Tressait 38 B2
Tretower 13 E4
Treyford 50 C3
Trimdon 31 D3
Trimsaran 6 B1
Tring 15 F3
Trinity 39 E2
Trochry 38 C3
Troedyrhiw 7 E1
Troon 33 E3
Troutbeck 29 F4
Troutbeck Bridge 29 F4
Trowbridge 8 B1
Trumpington 16 B2
Truro 3 F3
Trysull 54 A2
Tudweiliog 18 A3
Tummel Bridge 38 B2
Tunga 47 F2
Tunstall *Staffs.* **56 B3**
Tunstall *Suff.* 17 F2
Turner's Green 55 D4
Turners Hill 10 B3
Turnford 53 E1
Turriff 43 E2
Tutbury 20 C3
Tutnall 54 B4
Tutshill 7 F1
Tuxford 21 E1

Twatt 49 D3
Twechar 33 F1
Twechar 61 E1
Tweedmouth 35 E2
Tweedsmuir 34 B3
Twickenham 52 C4
Twiss Green 59 D2
Two Gates 55 E1
Twycross 55 F1
Twyford *Berks.* 15 E4
Twyford *Hants.* 9 E2
Twyn-yr-odyn 51 D2
Twynholm 28 C2
Twyning 14 B2
Tyburn 55 D2
Tye Common 53 H2
Tyldesley 59 D1
Tylers Green *Essex* **53 G1**
Tyndrum 37 F3
Tynemouth 31 D1
Tynemouth 60 B2
Tythegston 7 D2
Tywardreath 4 A3
Tywyn 12 C1

U

Uachdar 46 B2
Uckfield 10 C3
Uddingston 33 F2
Uddingston 61 E2
Uddington 34 A3
Uffculme 7 E4
Ufton 55 F5
Uig 40 B2
Ulbster 45 F2
Ulceby 27 D3
Ulgham 35 F4
Ullapool 41 D1
Ullenhall 55 D5
Ulleskelf 26 B2
Ulley 57 E4
Ulpha 29 E4
Ulsta 48 B2
Ulverston 24 C1
Umberleigh 6 C4
Unapool 44 B2
Underwood *Newport* **51 D3**
Undy 7 F2
Undy 51 E3
Unstone 21 D1
Upavon 8 C1
Uphampton 54 A5
Up Holland 25 D4
Up Holland 58 C1
Uplyme 5 F1
Up Marden 50 B3
Upminster 53 G3
Upper Aston 54 A2
Upper Boat 51 D1
Upper Camster 45 F2
Upper Catshill 54 B4
Upper Clatford 9 D2
Upper Eastern Green 55 E3
Upper Gornal 54 B2
Upper Halliford 52 B5
Upper Heyford 15 D2
Upper Knockando 42 C3
Upper Ludstone 54 A2
Upper Mitton 54 A4
Upper Norwood 53 E4
Upper Stoke 55 F3
Upper Tean 20 B2
Upper Tooting 52 D4
Uppingham 21 F4
Upshire 53 F1
Upton *Berks.* **52 A4**
Upton *Ches.* 19 F2
Upton *Ches.* **58 B5**
Upton *Dorset* 8 C3
Upton *Hants.* **50 A1**

Upton St. Leonards 14 B3
Upton upon Severn 14 B2
Upton Warren 54 B5
Urafirth 48 B2
Urlay Nook 60 A5
Urmston 25 D4
Urmston 59 E2
Ushaw Moor 30 C2
Usk 7 F1
Uttoxeter 20 C2
Uxbridge 10 A1
Uxbridge 52 B3
Uyeasound 48 C1

V

Valley 18 A1
Valsgarth 48 C1
Veensgarth 48 B3
Ventnor 9 E4
Verwood 8 C3
Vickerstown 24 B1
Vidlin 48 C2
Viewpark 33 F2
Viewpark 61 F2
Vigo 54 C1
Vigo Village 53 H5
Virginia Water 10 A2
Virginia Water 52 A5
Voe 48 B2

W

Waddesdon 15 E3
Waddington 21 F1
Wadebridge 4 A2
Wadhurst 10 C3
Wadsley Bridge 57 D3
Wadworth 57 F3
Wainfleet All Saints 22 B2
Wainhouse Corner 4 A1
Wakefield 26 A3
Wakefield 57 F2
Walberswick 17 F1
Walderslade 11 D2
Walderton 50 B3
Waldridge 60 A3
Wales 26 A4
Wales 57 E4
Walkden 59 E1
Walker 60 A2
Walkwood 54 C5
Wall *Staffs.* **55 D1**
Wallasey 19 E1
Wall Heath 54 A3
Wallingford 15 E4
Wallington *Gt.Lon.* **52 D5**
Wallington *Hants.* **50 C2**
Walls 48 B3
Wallsend 31 D1
Wallsend 60 B2
Wallyford 34 C1
Walmer 11 F2
Walmley 55 D2
Walsall 26 B1
Walsall 54 C2
Walsall Wood 54 C1
Walsgrave on Sowe 55 F3
Waltham 27 D4
Waltham Abbey 16 B4
Waltham Abbey 53 E1
Waltham Chase 50 C1
Waltham Forest 53 E2
Waltham on the Wolds 21 E3
Walthamstow 53 E3
Walton *Mers.* **58 A2**
Walton-in-Gordano 51 E4
Walton-le-Dale 25 D3
Walton-on-Naze 17 E3
Walton-on-Thames 52 C5
Walton on Thames 10 A2

Wandsworth 52 D4
Wanstead 53 F3
Wantage 15 D4
Wappenbury 55 F5
Warboys 16 A1
Warburton 59 D3
Warcop 30 A3
Ward End 55 D3
Wardington 15 D2
Ware 16 B3
Wareham 8 B4
Wargrave 15 E4
Wark 30 B1
Warkworth 35 F4
Warley 54 C3
Warlingham 10 B2
Warmfield 57 F2
Warmington 15 D2
Warminster 8 B1
Warren *Ches.* **59 F4**
Warrenby 60 C4
Warrington 19 F1
Warrington 59 D3
Warsash 50 B2
Warslow 20 C1
Warsop 21 D1
Warton *Warks.* **55 E1**
Warton (Carnforth) *Lancs.* 24 C1
Warwick 14 C1
Warwick 55 E5
Warwick Bridge 29 F2
Wasbister 49 E2
Washingborough 21 F1
Washington *T. & W.* 31 D2
Washington *T. & W.* **60 B3**
Wass 26 B1
Watchet 7 E4
Watchgate 30 A4
Waterbeach 16 B1
Waterfoot *E.Renf.* **61 D3**
Waterloo *Mers.* **58 A2**
Waterlooville 9 E3
Waterlooville 50 A3
Water Orton 20 C4
Water Orton 55 D2
Waterside *Bucks.* **52 A1**
Waterside *E.Dun.* **61 E1**
Watford *Herts.* 16 A4
Watford *Herts.* **52 C2**
Wath upon Dearne 26 A4
Watlington 15 E4
Watnall 56 C1
Watten 45 F2
Watton 23 D4
Watton-at-Stone 16 A3
Wattston 61 F2
Waverton *Ches.* **58 B5**
Wealdstone 52 C3
Weatheroak Hill 54 C4
Weaverham 19 F1
Weaverham 59 D4
Webheath 54 C5
Weddington 55 F2
Wedmore 7 F3
Wednesbury 20 B4
Wednesbury 54 B2
Wednesfield 54 B1
Weedon Bec 15 E1
Weeford 55 D1
Weem 38 B2
Weldon 21 F4
Welham Green 52 D1
Wellesbourne 14 C1
Well Hill 53 F5
Welling 53 F4
Wellingborough 15 F1
Wellington *Shrop.* 20 A3
Wellington *Som.* 7 E4

Wells 7 F3
Wells-next-the-Sea 23 D2
Wellsborough 55 F1
Welney 22 B4
Welshpool 13 E1
Welton *Lincs.* 21 F1
Welwyn 16 A3
Welwyn Garden City 16 A3
Wem 19 F3
Wembdon 7 E3
Wembley 52 C3
Wemyss Bay 33 E1
Wendens Ambo 16 B2
Wendover 15 F3
Wendron 3 E3
Wennington *Gt.Lon.* **53 G3**
Wensley 30 C4
Wentworth *S.Yorks.* 26 A4
Wentworth *S.Yorks.* **57 D3**
Wenvoe 51 D2
Weobley 13 F3
Wereham 22 C4
Wergs 54 A1
Werrington *Staffs.* **56 C4**
Wervin 58 B4
West Ashling 50 C4
West Auckland 30 C3
West Bergholt 17 D3
West Boldon 60 B2
Westbourne *W.Suss.* 50 B4
West Bridgford 21 E2
West Bridgford 56 C2
West Bromwich 20 B4
West Bromwich 54 C2
Westbury 8 B1
Westbury on Trym 51 F4
West Byfleet 52 B5
West Calder 34 A2
West Coker 7 F4
Westcott 10 A2
West Dean *W.Suss.* **50 C3**
West Derby 58 A2
West Drayton *Gt.Lon.* **52 B4**
West End *Hants.* **50 B1**
West End (Bisley) *Surr.* **52 A5**
West End (Esher) *Surr.* **52 C5**
Westerdale 45 E2
Westergate 9 F3
Westerham 10 C2
Wester Parkgate 29 E1
Westfield 11 D4
West Garforth 57 F1
Westgate 30 B2
Westgate Hill 57 E2
West Grinstead 10 B3
West Haddon 15 E1
West Hagley 54 B3
West Hallam 56 B1
West Ham 53 F3
Westhampnett 50 C4
West Harptree 7 F3
Westhead 58 B1
West Heath *W.Mid.* **54 C4**
Westhill 43 E4
West Hill *N.W.Som.* **51 E4**
West Horndon 53 H3
Westhoughton 59 D1
West Hyde 52 B2
West Itchenor 50 B4
West Kilbride 33 E2
West Kingsdown 53 G5
West Kirby 19 E1
West Knapton 26 C1
West Lavington 8 B1
Westleigh *Gt.Man.* **59 D1**
Westleton 17 F1
West Linton 34 B2
West Lulworth 8 B4
West Malling 11 D2
West Marden 50 B3
West Meon 9 E2

West Mersea 17 D3
West Molesey 52 C5
West Monkton 7 E4
West Moors 8 C3
Westness 49 E2
West Norwood 53 E4
Weston *Ches.* **56 A3**
Weston *Ches.* **58 C3**
· Weston *Dorset* 8 A4
Weston *Staffs.* 20 B3
Weston-in-Gordano 51 E4
Weston-super-Mare 7 F3
Weston Coyney 56 C4
Weston Green *Surr.* **52 C5**
Weston Point 58 B3
**Weston under Wetherley
55 F5**
Westonzoyland 7 F4
West Park *Mers.* **58 C2**
Westruther 35 D2
West Somerton 23 F4
West Stoke 50 C4
West Tarbert 32 C2
West Thorney 50 B4
West Thurrock 53 G4
West Tilbury 53 H4
Westward Ho! 6 B4
West Wickham *Gt.Lon.* **53 E5**
West Winch 22 C3
Westwood Heath 55 E4
West Wycombe 15 E4
West Yell 48 B2
Wetheral 29 F2
Wetherby 26 A2
Wetley Rocks 56 C4
Weybridge 10 A2
Weybridge 52 B5
Weymouth 8 A4
Whaley Bridge 25 F4
Whalton 30 C1
Whaplode 22 A3
Wharncliffe Side 57 D3
Wharton *Ches.* **59 D5**
Whauphill 28 B2
Wheatley Hill 31 D2
Wheaton Aston 20 B3
Wheddon Cross 7 D3
Wheelock 56 A3
Whelpley Hill 52 B1
Wherwell 9 D2
Whickham 60 A2
Whiddon Down 4 C1
Whifflet 61 F2
Whimple 5 E1
Whiston *Mers.* **58 B2**
Whiston *S.Yorks.* 26 A4
Whiston *S.Yorks.* **57 E4**
Whitburn *W.Loth.* 34 A2
Whitburn *T. & W.* **60 C2**
Whitby *Ches.* **58 A4**
Whitby *N.Yorks.* 31 F3
Whitchurch *Bucks.* 15 E3
Whitchurch *Cardiff* 7 D2
Whitchurch *Cardiff* **51 D2**
Whitchurch *Hants.* 9 E1
Whitchurch *Shrop.* 19 F3
Whitecraig 34 C1
Whitecraig 61 F4
Whitefield *Gt.Man.* **59 F1**
Whitegate 59 D5
Whitehall 49 F2
Whitehaven 29 D3
Whitehill 9 F2
Whitehills 43 F2
Whiteley 50 C2
Whiteley Village 52 B5
White Moor 56 A1
Whiterashes 43 E4
Whitfield 11 F2

Whithorn 28 B2
Whiting Bay 33 D3
Whitkirk 57 F1
Whitland 12 A4
Whitley Bay 31 D1
Whitley Bay 60 B1
Whitlock's End 55 D4
Whitmore *Staffs.* 56 B4
Whitnash 15 D1
Whitnash 55 F5
Whitson 51 D3
Whitstable 11 E2
Whittingham 35 E4
Whittington *Shrop.* 19 E3
Whittington (Kinver) *Staffs.* 54 A3
Whittington (Lichfield) *Staffs.* 55 D1
Whittlesey 22 A4
Whitton *Stock.* 60 A4
Whitworth 25 E3
Wibsey 57 D1
Wick *Bridg.* 7 D2
Wick *High.* 45 F2
Wick *S.Glos.* 14 A4
Wick *W.Suss.* 10 A4
Wickersley 26 A4
Wickersley 57 E3
Wickford 11 D1
Wickham *Hants.* 9 E3
Wickham *Hants.* 50 C1
Wickham Market 17 E2
Wickwar 14 A4
Widecombe in the Moor 4 C2
Wide Open 60 A1
Widford 16 B3
Widnes 19 F1
Widnes 58 C3
Wigan 25 D3
Wigan 58 C1
Wigginton *Staffs.* 55 E1
Wigmore 13 F2
Wigston 21 E4
Wigthorpe 57 F4
Wigton 29 F2
Wigtown 28 B2
Wilcrick 51 E3
Wilden *H. & W.* 54 A4
Wildhill 52 D1
Wilford 56 C2
Willaston (Wirral) *Ches.* 19 E1
Willaston (Wirral) *Ches.* 58 A4
Willenhall (Coventry) *W.Mid.* 55 F4
Willenhall (Walsall) *W.Mid.* 54 B2
Willesden 52 D3
Willingale 53 G1
Willingdon 10 C4
Willingham 16 B1
Willington *Derbys.* 20 C2
Willington *Dur.* 30 C3
Willington *T. & W.* 60 B2
Willington Corner 58 C5
Williton 7 E3
Willoughby 22 B1
Wilmington *Kent* 10 C1
Wilmington *Kent* 53 G4
Wilmslow 25 E4
Wilmslow 59 F3
Wilnecote 55 E1
Wilton *R. & C.* 60 C4
Wilton *Wilts.* 8 C2
Wimbledon 52 D4
Wimblington 22 B4
Wimborne Minster 8 C3
Wincanton 8 B2
Wincham 59 D4
Winchburgh 34 B1
Winchcombe 14 B2

Winchelsea 11 D3
Winchester 9 E2
Winchmore Hill *Gt.Lon.* 53 E2
Wincobank 57 D3
Windermere 29 F4
Windlesham 52 A5
Windley 56 A1
Windley Meadows 56 A1
Windsor 10 A1
Windsor 52 A4
Windygates 39 D4
Winford 7 F2
Wing 15 F3
Wingate 31 D2
Wingates *Gt.Man.* 59 D1
Wingerworth 21 D1
Wingham 11 F2
Winkfield 10 A1
Winkfield 52 A4
Winkleigh 4 C1
Winnersh 9 F1
Winscombe 7 F3
Winsford *Ches.* 19 F2
Winsford *Ches.* 59 D5
Winsley 8 B1
Winslow 15 E2
Winsor 50 A1
Winston 30 C3
Winterbourne 14 A4
Winterbourne Abbas 8 A4
Winterley 56 A3
Wintershill 50 C1
Winterton 26 C3
Winton 30 B3
Winwick *Ches.* 59 D2
Wirksworth 20 C2
Wisbech 22 B3
Wishaw 34 A2
Wishaw *N.Lan.* 61 F3
Wishaw *Warks.* 55 D2
Wistanstow 13 F2
Wistaston 20 A2
Witham 16 C3
Witheridge 7 D4
Witherley 55 F2
Withernsea 27 E3
Withington *Gt.Man.* 59 F2
Withington Green 59 F4
Witley 9 F2
Witney 15 D3
Wittering 21 F3
Witton Gilbert 30 C2
Wiveliscombe 7 E4
Wivenhoe 17 D3
Woburn 15 F2
Woburn Sands 15 F2
Woking 10 A2
Wokingham 9 F1
Wold Newton 27 D1
Wollaston *Nhants.* 15 F1
Wollaston *W.Mid.* 54 A3
Wolsingham 30 C2
Wolston 15 D1
Wolverhampton 20 B4
Wolverhampton 54 B2
Wolverley *H. & W.* 20 B4
Wolverley *H. & W.* 54 A4
Wolverton *Bucks.* 15 E2
Wolverton *Warks.* 55 E5
Wolviston 60 B4
Wombourne 20 B4
Wombourne 54 A2
Wombwell 26 A4
Wooburn 10 A1
Woodborough 21 E2
Woodbridge 17 E2
Woodcote 15 E4
Woodend *W.Suss.* 50 C4
Wood End (Redditch) *Warks.* 55 D4

Wood End (Tamworth) *Warks.* 55 E2
Woodford *Gt.Lon.* 53 F2
Woodford *Gt.Man.* 59 F3
Woodford Bridge 53 F2
Woodford Green 53 F2
Woodgate *H.& W.* 54 B5
Woodgate *W.Mid.* 54 B3
Wood Green 53 E2
Woodhall Spa 22 A1
Woodham *Surr.* 52 B5
Wood Hayes 54 B1
Woodhouse *S.Yorks.* 57 E4
Woodingdean 10 B4
Woodland 30 C3
Woodlands *Hants.* 50 A1
Woodlesford 57 F2
Woodley 15 E4
Woodmancote *W.Suss.* 50 B4
Woodmansey 27 D2
Woodplumpton 25 D2
Woodsetts 57 F4
Woodside *Berks.* 52 A4
Woodside *Herts.* 52 D1
Woodside *W.Mid.* 54 B3
Woodstock 15 D3
Woodton 23 E4
Woodville 20 C3
Wool 8 B4
Woolacombe 6 B3
Wooler 35 E3
Woolmere Green 54 B5
Woolston *Ches.* 19 F1
Woolston *Ches.* 59 D3
Woolston *Hants.* 50 B1
Woolton 58 B3
Woolwich 53 F4
Woore 56 A4
Wootton 15 F2
Wootton Bassett 14 C4
Wootton Wawen 55 D5
Worcester 14 B1
Worcester Park 52 D5
Wordsley 54 A3
Worfield 20 A4
Workington 29 E3
Worksop 21 E1
Worlds End 50 A3
Wormit 39 D3
Wormley *Herts.* 53 E1
Worplesdon 10 A2
Worrall 57 D3
Worsley 59 E1
Worth 10 B3
Worthing 10 A4
Wortley *S.Yorks.* 57 D3
Wotton-under-Edge 14 A4
Woughton on the Green 15 F2
Wragby 22 A1
Wrangle 22 B2
Wraxall *N.W.Som.* 51 E4
Wraysbury 52 B4
Wrea Green 24 C3
Wrekenton 60 A3
Wrelton 31 F4
Wrenthorpe 57 F2
Wrexham 19 E2
Wrinehill 56 A4
Wrington 7 F2
Writtle 16 C4
Wrotham Hill 53 H5
Wrotham Park 52 D2
Wroughton 14 C4
Wroxhall 55 E4
Wyberton 22 A2
Wychbold 54 B5
Wye 11 E2
Wyke *W.Yorks.* 57 D2
Wylde Green 55 D2
Wylye 8 C2

Wymering 50 A4
Wymondham *Leics.* 21 F3
Wymondham *Norf.* 23 E4
Wyre Piddle 14 B2
Wythall 14 C1
Wythall 54 C4

Y

Yapton 10 A4
Yardley 55 D3
Yarm 31 D3
Yarm 60 B5
Yarmouth 9 D4
Yarnton 15 D3
Yarrow 34 C3
Yate 14 A4
Yateley 9 F1
Yatton 7 F2
Yaxley 22 A4
Yeading 52 C3
Yeadon 25 F2
Yealmpton 4 C3
Yeovil 7 F4
Yeovilton 7 F4
Yiewsley 52 B4
Ynysddu 7 E1
Yoker 61 D2
York 26 B2
Youlgreave 20 C1
Yoxall 20 C3
Yoxford 17 F1
Ysbyty Ystwyth 12 C2
Ystalyfera 6 C1
Ystrad 7 D1
Ystradgynlais 6 C1

Z

Zennor 3 D3